The Spirit of Joy:

How to live a psycho-spiritually integrated Christian life

JOSEPH MALANCHARUVIL

Moraga, California, USA
June 8, 2018
Feast of the Most Sacred Heart of Jesus

Print ISBN 978-1-54393-825-8
eBook ISBN 978-1-54393-826-5

TO THE SOCIETY OF JESUS, ESPECIALLY THE KERALA JESUITS, IN GRATEFUL ACKNOWLEDGMENT OF THEIR CONTRIBUTIONS TO THE SPIRITUAL AND EDUCATIONAL FORMATION OF THE AUTHOR.

FOREWORD

(To the first edition)

Scientific psychology and spirituality have a history of a love-hate relationship. Much water has flowed under the bridge since Sigmund Freud, the founder of Psychoanalysis, declared religion and spirituality as a mental defense, an "illusion of the mind." Increasingly, psychology and religion have come to recognize that they are not inimical or opposed to each other; on the contrary, they are highly complementary to each other in enhancing and enriching the quality of human life. While scientific psychology has demythologized and removed superstitious understanding of the human psyche, it has also increasingly demonstrated through ongoing research that religion and spirituality are complementary contributors to human homeostasis and inner peace. It is in this context of a genuine dialogue between psychology and spirituality, *Psycho-spiritual Integration* makes a serious contribution to our understanding.

Dr. Malancharuvil's considerable scientific and clinical experience along with his substantial philosophical and theological training provides innovative depth in his formulations of psycho-spiritual integration. His writings, especially the chapter on spiritual discernment, reveal his Jesuit education. In a crisp and pithy manner, he summarizes the essential foundations of modern psychology as well as Christian spirituality. As I read the book, I remember his conversations with me and the valuable insights he provided in my formation as a psychologist and consecrated religious. His gentleness, depth of scholarship, and above all spiritual integration left an indelible impression on me.

I am delighted that my Sisters at Sacred Heart Congregation contributed to the inspiration of this book. They are the first recipients of this valuable writing. I do not doubt that Dr. Malancharuvil's contribution to this vital subject will bear great fruits and will be of invaluable assistance to both the general public, and especially to those in charge of spiritually guiding others.

TESLIN JOSEPH, S.H., PH.D., M.PHIL. M.S. (PSYCHOPHARMACOLOGY)
MAY 2015, TRIVANDRUM, KERALA.

TABLE OF CONTENTS

FOREWORD vii

PREFACE.. 1

CHAPTER 1
Introduction 3

CHAPTER 2
Psychological Foundations 7

    The structure of the human psyche...7

    Perceptual and Cognitive processes...9

    Emotional processes...10

    Motivation 13

    Object Relations and Cognitive Triad..13

    Personality 14

    Self-Efficacy...16

    Achievement Motivation..17

    Stages of Psychosocial Development 18

    Psychological Programming 22

    Mental Illness...24

    Psychotherapy versus spiritual direction...26

CHAPTER 3
Psychosexual Development...29

CHAPTER 4
Foundations of Christian spirituality..36

CHAPTER 5
Essential pre-requisites for psycho-spiritual integration.................39

CHAPTER 6
Essential Elements ofPsycho-spiritual Integration 51

Mindfulness..51

Authenticity..53

Spontaneity..55

Intimacy...56

Autonomy...57

Openness 60

CHAPTER 7

Discernment of the Spirits 62

The Spirit of God and His good Angels...63

The Evil Spirits 65

The Spirit of the "World" 65

The Human Spirit 68

The spiritual States and Related Movements 71

The "evil" or corrupt state...71

The Tepid State..72

The Militant State...74

CHAPTER 8

Practicing Integration 81

Training our brain: 82

Spiritual Exercises and hypnotic phenomenon: 83

Alpha-Theta Self Training 87

Aids to contemplative prayer: 90

CHAPTER 9

Exercises 92

Integrated life on a daily basis: some practical steps........................92

Keeping the House Clean 97

Daily Self Examination 99

Establishing a place of consultation 101

Discernment before making decision..103

Achieving a goal...105

Overcoming a spiritual obstacle or challenge................................106

A method of contemplating an incident in the Scripture
(adapted from the Spiritual Exercises of St. Ignatius Loyola).......................... 108

A method of discursive meditation on a scripture passage 110

A meditation to increase faith:.. 112

A meditation to increase Hope in times of trial:.. 114

Accessing the Divine Counselor: a contemplative exercise in discernment 116

A lesson from the Master Himself on Christian love 118

Walk in the Spirit.. 120

A Meditation for healing the body.. 122

Healing the trauma of childhood sexual abuse 124

CHAPTER 10
Experiencing God in all things:

The spirituality of the laity for the 21st century 128

PREFACE

Psycho-spiritual integration has two interlinked components: psychological and spiritual. The harmonious balancing of these components is the theme of this book: *The Spirit of Joy, How to live a psycho-spiritually integrated life*. It describes practical ways to arrive at genuine and enduring psycho-spiritual integration and happiness. Everlasting joy is our destiny. "These things I have spoken to you, that my joy may be in you, and that your joy may be full" (Jn. 15:11). We arrive at this inner joy and enduring peace through a meandering and sometimes steep journey of purification, carrying our cross to the mountain-top, together with the Lord, until we have overcome evil and death. The Lord assures us of victory as we fix our vision on Him and His unfailing promises. We may falter and fall, but we do not succumb or lose hope. This journey of suffering is not inconsistent with inner joy; on the contrary, it helps us to deepen our love, understanding of life, and psycho-spiritual integration (Rom. 8:35-39). Enduring happiness, joy, contentment, and peace are the fruits of an integrated life. "But the fruit of the Spirit is love, joy, peace, patience, kindness, goodness, faithfulness, gentleness, self-control; against such, there is no law" (Gal. 5:22,23). We are asked to "Rejoice in the Lord always, again I will say, Rejoice" (Phil. 4:4.). "I came that they may have life, and have it abundantly" (Jn. 10:10). Letting the Spirit of God pervade our life is the way to genuine freedom and lasting joy. "And the peace of God, which passes all understanding, will keep your hearts and your minds in Christ Jesus" (Phil. 4:7).

Readers may start with the last three chapters of the book if they are just interested in the practical exercises of psycho-spiritual integration. The early discussions are foundational and may prove to be very useful to deepen the understanding of the psychological and spiritual dynamics of integration. The section on spiritual discernment is particularly important and very crucial, as making wise choices is at the heart of an integrated life. The last part is dedicated to the laity, detailing proven and simple steps to living an integrated life on a daily basis within the family.

The Religious Sisters of the Sacred Heart, especially Sister Doctor Teslin Joseph, S.H., the Provincial Superior, initially inspired the author to write this book. The Sisters wanted a month-long course on psycho-spiritual integration. I prepared the original as a manual for a course in psycho-spiritual integration. The first edition was sold out. I have made several changes and additions in the second edition profiting from the feedback and recommendations of several readers of the first edition. I thank the Sisters, especially Sr. Dr. Teslin, for their kind encouragement, support, and feedback.

I dedicate this book gratefully to the Society of Jesus, especially to the members of the Kerala Jesuit Province. I received my spiritual formation, philosophical, theological, and psychological education from outstanding and holy Jesuits, including those at the Loyola University of Chicago, where I received my doctoral degree in clinical psychology. Additionally, I want to remember gratefully and fondly my spiritual director and mentor, Father Anthony De Mello, S.J. who had a profound influence in my spiritual formation. I thank those who read the manuscript and gave valuable feedback, especially Dr. George Nedy, Dr. Les Berkes, and Dr. Sheila Maliekel.

Without the patient endurance, personal sacrifice, and quiet encouragement of Kathleen, my spouse, and life-companion, this book would not have materialized. My daughters, Elizabeth and Kiran, have been asking me to write this book for a long time. I am grateful that they persisted until I did.

It is my sincere and prayerful hope that *The Spirit of Joy, How to Live a Psycho-spiritually Integrated Life* become a helpful resource book for many who long for the indwelling of the Holy Spirit in their lives, making them happy, joyful, and everlastingly peaceful.

June 8, 2018, Feast of the Most Sacred Heart of Jesus, California, USA.

CHAPTER 1

Introduction

Knowing ourselves as God's beloved creation leads us to the worship of the mystery and unfathomable love of God. In this context, we discuss psycho-spiritual integration. What we are searching for is embedded deep within and among us; God's reign is within us, in our midst (Lk. 17:21). The human psyche is the locus of human awareness, reflection, and decision making. Without self-awareness, there is no culture, morality, or human action. It is the place where physiology, psychology, and spirituality meet; it is also the locus of our conscious interaction with God. Therefore, it is of crucial importance that we understand the dynamics of the human psyche to be able to integrate the psychological and spiritual aspects of our being. Psycho-spiritual integration, no matter how it was named historically, has been and will be the central and personal struggle of all humans.

The Catholic teaching is that a human being is an embodied spirit," that is a soul which expresses itself in a body, a body informed by an immortal spirit," a unity of physical, psychological, and spiritual systems in one being (See John Paul II, The Apostolic Exhortation on the Family, *Familiaris Consortio*, no. 11.). These systems are intimately connected and interact together to form an integrated unity of being. Therefore, psycho-spiritual integration (PSI) is the harmonious balancing of the psychological and spiritual aspects of a human being. It is rooted in self-awareness guided by faith, loving and honest interpersonal relationships, discernment of the Spirits, and spiritual experiences in such a way that it continues to nourish, enhance and maintain inner peace and openness to life. Psycho-spiritual integration calls for an active awareness and management of these interacting and intimately related systems at work within the unity of the human person. PSI is an ongoing process throughout life and is not a fixated outcome. Everyone experiences integration in some manner. Therefore, the discussion is not of the presence of integration, but of its ongoing enhancement, quality, potency, and sustainability. The human being is a finite energy system; the forces at work within need to be brought continuously into balance and homeostasis. The integrative process is the ground of human homeostasis and protects it from disorganization and disintegration. Integration happens both unconsciously and through conscious efforts. When the integrative process falls apart or is inadequate, confusion, mental illnesses, and severe behavioral disorders may result.

We start with our fundamental belief in the crucial role of religion and spirituality in living an integrated life. Religious quest is an intrinsic motivation of human beings as history has abundantly proven. *Homo sapiens* is also *homo religiosus.* Our rational nature and intelligence, limited in its capacity, is unbounded in its search for knowledge of the mysteries of life and reality. We have not unraveled all the secrets of existence. Secondly, science by its very nature and method is limited to empirically verifiable aspects of reality. Existential questions of meaning and purpose of life are beyond the purview of empirical methods. It is our relationship to what is transcendent that prompts our innate religious instinct. Through this instinct, humankind has created myths, images, concepts, etc. of the transcendent reality. The natural moral sense of distinguishing right from wrong, the perpetual human struggle with good and evil, and the perennial hope that good will eventually overcome evil, and justice will prevail at the end, etc. are the genuine sentiments that guided humanity throughout history.

Christians know and believe that God has answered the religious quest of humanity, fulfilling all spiritual longings. Christianity is neither the product of *human* imagination and speculation nor is it a mere *ration*al answer to the religious pursuit. It is God's definitive and historical initiative with us, fulfilling the inherent human need for God. It is not the mythology of antiquity, however profound and meaningful such had been. While humans were searching for God, God had already been pursuing them.

God met us in flesh and blood in Jesus Christ, by entering and becoming part of our history.

> *And the Word became flesh and dwelt among us, full of grace and truth; we have beheld his glory, glory as of the only begotten Son from the Father (Jn1: 14).*

> *In this, the love of God was made manifest among us, that God sent his only Son into the world so that we might live through him (1Jn. 4:9)*

God has indeed become part of our history by pitching his tent in our midst. The Lord has demonstrated who He is, by His Word, proven correct by His deeds in our history. Jesus' life, deeds, death, and triumphant resurrection have shown to us that He is genuinely the incarnate Word of God, the Logos, which gives existence and meaning to everything that is. Jesus Christ is not *a* founder of *a* religion; He is *the* definitive fulfillment of all religious aspirations. For Christians this is not a philosophical argument or conclusion, it is a historical as well as meta-historical fact that demands response in a commitment of faith, albeit the fact that in Christianity the highest and noblest philosophical findings of man have been rationally incorporated into teaching. It is faith that searches for the reason and then transcends and fulfills it; it is not the human reason that finds faith, because, while reason cannot contradict Him, God is beyond human reason or effort.

> *"No one has ever seen God; the only-begotten Son, who is in the bosom of the Father, he has made him known" (Jn. 1:18).*

In such a context, for a believing Christian, an integrated human life is impossible to achieve without Jesus Christ. For a Christian, an atheistic or non-religious integration is an irrelevant discussion. However, for those who have not discovered this truth, such a debate could be meaningful and even productive.

> *"The glory of God is the man fully alive, and the life of man is the vision of God. If the revelation of God through creation already*

brings life to all living beings on the earth, how much more will the manifestation of the Father by the Word bring life to those who see God" (St. Irenaeus AH-IV, 20, 7).

Christianity does not reject science and its marvelous achievements. On the contrary, Christianity affirms and celebrates human science and its success. An anti-scientific, anti-rational attitude contradicts God's purpose in endowing human beings with intelligence and the necessary obligations to explore, contemplate, and master nature. Scientific psychology is no exception. The human psyche is the conscious locus of the interaction of psychological and spiritual realities. Without our God-given psyche, we cannot consciously interact with God. God wants us to communicate with Him consciously with awareness and deliberation. Understanding the nature and dynamics of our mind enhances our ability to discern the spiritual realities of our life. As we shall see later in detail, the human psyche is the battleground for the souls of humankind. Our spiritual struggles manifest in our awareness. There is neither morality nor contemplation without awareness. There is no genuine freedom without virtue. Indeed, the distinguishing human characteristic is the ability for self-determination which is impossible without consciousness of self and our surroundings. Psychological science contributes substantially to the evolving understanding of our psychic structure and dynamics. It is obvious, then, that psychology and spirituality are highly complementary to each other.

CHAPTER 2

Psychological Foundations

The structure of the human psyche

Several theories have been proposed to describe the structure of the human psyche. For our purposes, regardless of a particular theoretical framework, we shall stay with those that are commonly agreed upon, demonstrated by universal experience and applicability. In scientific psychology, the term psyche has been used to refer to the processes within the individual that give rise to the psychological phenomena such as emotions, thoughts, behavior, and personality. In recent times the cognitive psychologists have preferred the word "mind" to "psyche." As Carl Jung has clarified, the psyche should not be confused with the soul; the former is a process while the latter is a principle of being.

Sigmund Freud revolutionized the understanding of the structure of the human psyche by proposing that two-thirds of our mental functioning is hidden from our awareness. He termed this hidden part of our psyche the Unconscious. The aspect of the Unconscious that is more readily accessible is called the Subconscious. The Unconscious profoundly influences the way we perceive, behave, relate, and experience life. Additionally, Freud proposed that our awareness is tailored to suit the hidden desires, emotions, motivations, etc. by powerful psychological dynamics he termed mental *defenses*. A dramatic example of a mental defense is conversion-reaction, such as hysterical blindness or paralysis without physiological causes. The primary purpose of the psychological defenses is to protect the individual from experiencing massive and paralyzing anxiety which is inherent to the human condition. To be aware that we may not be aware is the beginning of psychological wisdom!

Dynamically, according to Freud, the human psyche is known to have three distinct processes, the *Id*, *Ego*, and the *Superego*. As an infant one starts with a cauldron of desires, impulses, needs, drives, etc. These uninhibited and uncultivated natural processes are termed the *Id*. However, early on in life, we come to recognize that we must regulate these fundamental movements and behave consistently with the demands of reality and society to be able to function effectively. The *ego* is the process that negotiates the requirements of reality and societal expectations in the context of our natural impulses. The *superego* forms as we internalize the values and norms of the society. The balancing of these three systems creates the psychological dynamics of the mind.

In this context, the important concept of *conscience* needs to be discussed. Conscience has been described and defined in different ways throughout history. While there are serious variations in figuring out the origin, nature, development, and dynamics of conscience, there is relatively less dispute in describing conscience as the normative light that guides the free choices of human beings in issues of morality. In that sense, conscience is an essential part of the Superego. The moral values and the internalized norms of behavior approve or disapprove one's behavior. We have the ability to go against the promptings of our conscience. Acting against one's conscience tends to create internal disquiet and feelings of guilt and remorse. However, in certain circumstances, habitual ignoring of the promptings of one's conscience can dull the person's sense of guilt or remorse. A falsely or inadequately formed conscience can cause false guilt or lack of remorse. An extreme example would be the absence of guilt in the psyche of a person with a severe personality defect such as psychopathy. It is also possible that a person develops an oppressive Superego that leads to an overly sensitive conscience and scrupulosity. In this context it is important to note that some develop undue guilt regarding certain "unwanted" emotions that arise in their awareness. They treat these emotions as if they were actions. Emotions, as we discuss later in this chapter, are amoral. Deliberate actions, omissions, and the decisions that lead to such are the subject of morality. Spontaneously arising emotions, no matter how repugnant they may be perceived to be, are only the context of choosing actions. Until one has decided to act on an emotion, there are no moral imputations. In fact, certain "undue" emotions and the temptations to act them out could be the very occasions and opportunities to practice moral restraint, virtue, and good character.

Persons with a healthy integration of the three structures of the psyche are generally relaxed and self-acceptant. Such individuals permit awareness of their emotions and are in control of their actions. They, as a rule, adhere to the demands of their conscience. They know that failures are part of being human; with self-compassion, forgiveness, and a determination to improve, they move forward celebrating life.

Genetic and hereditary programming endows a human being with innate capacities. Among these, three functions are particularly crucial in the integrative process: first, sensory, perceptual, intellectual, and intuitive abilities, enhanced by reasoning and insight, leading to cognition, understanding, and wisdom; second, the ability to experience and express emotions; third, the freedom to choose and act. These highly complex processes require considerable elaboration; however, we shall limit our discussion to the essential elements especially relevant to the integrative processes.

Perceptual and Cognitive processes

Cognitive processes start with the innate sensory as well as putative cognitive mechanisms. Employing our five senses coupled with the organismic and proprioceptive sensation of self, we experience the empirical world and ourselves as they stimulate our senses. Through similarity, contrast, and contiguity, we categorize and catalog the myriad sensations and percepts into cognition. These cognitions are further assimilated and expanded by the intellect through logical reasoning, intuition, and insight. At the high levels of abstraction, we develop beliefs about ourselves, others, the world around us, and life itself. Clusters of beliefs, in turn, become systematized into themes, called schemata. Once such is formed and confirmed by repeated experience, they are highly resistant to change. These cognitive systems, in turn, qualify and influence the way we foresee, process, and assimilate new events. Thus, the cognitive structures reflect an essential part of a person's personality-structure and style. So many things can go wrong at every stage of these complex processes. For example, at the sensory level we are subject to sensory disorders and errors such as illusion or hallucination; at the perceptual and cognitive levels we are liable to distortions, misinterpretations of data, etc.; at the reasoning level, illogicalities can abound. A well-integrated person is keenly aware of these pitfalls and develops a healthy skepticism about his or her cognitive conclusions.

Some of our knowledge are related to our very survival or critical needs. Such cognitions are invested ("cathected") with powerful emotions and affective energy. Cognitions and emotions are mutually generative. For example, an untrusting and suspicious view of others can lead to paranoid feelings of distrust and hostility.

Emotional processes

Feelings, emotions, and affective states are challenging to define as there are scores of definitions given in the literature. Emotions are surges of internal energy that is subjectively experienced as feelings, and call for some form of expression. Emotions involve a physiological and psychological arousal in the context of internal or external events or objects. Neurotransmitters, hormones, and physiological states have a direct influence on emotional arousals and vice versa. It is also true that emotions are aroused as a direct result of the meanings given to the perceptual and cognitive conclusions. Interpersonal and societal conditioning plays an essential role in how we learn to experience, regulate, and manage emotional arousals. All emotions have objects, whether the objects are consciously perceived or not. Emotions have been classified in varied ways by several theorists. Here we do not need to list or describe the multiple categories and spectrum of human emotions. Some of these emotions are slow in coming and in dissipating such as sadness and melancholy, while some are experienced as volatile and fast moving, such as anger and delight. Some impel us to action such as anger or fear, while some prompt us to inaction, such as feelings of ambivalence, fatigue, laziness or sadness. Suffice it to say that without emotions, the human being's life is experientially jejune, utterly impoverished, and as good as dead. Feelings are flesh and blood of psychic life. The queen of all emotions is love, which at its purest form culminates in the act of total self-giving and the joy of mystical union with the other...Experiencing love, both in receiving and giving it, is the most fulfilling emotional need of a human being. A child will not survive or flourish without it; an adult's life becomes meaningless and entirely impoverished without love.

Sustained affective states are called moods. Affect is to mood as the weather is to season. Moods may arise as a result of neurotransmitter regulations in the brain or other physiological states such as bipolar mood disorder. Moods are also often connected to patterns and styles of thinking. Because of this, some theorists consider specific mood problems such as exogenous (reactive, situational) depression as a result of thought-problems. Self-deprecatory beliefs or hostile prejudices towards others can, in turn, evoke emotions of self-loathing or hatred and fear of others. We also know that certain moods can evoke congruent thoughts, thus creating a vicious cycle.

Cognition and emotions are twins, distinct but intimately related. Cognition can evoke emotions and vice versa. The affective valence of cognition depends on how they associate in memory with feelings. Perceptions, thoughts, and beliefs can have significant emotional overtones depending on the meaning given to the experiences that created them. However emotional upheaval can sometimes hinder reality processing, consequently clouding understanding. Emotions are the powerful horses that drive the chariot in power; but the wise and courageous charioteer who guides and directs the horses is the understanding, awareness and the will of the person. When the emotions take over the control without the careful guidance of self, the result is chaos and destruction. It is equally valid that thought without emotional power is essentially unmoving. Experiences that correlate highly to the safety, attachments, nourishment, and development of the individual have a greater affective valence, because of their immediate significance for survival and growth.

While it is common to categorize emotions into positive and negative in terms of how they feel and what they prompt us to do, they do not carry an inherent moral value per se. Emotional arousals are not necessarily deliberate or willful. As a rule, emotions may emerge without conscious effort. Emotional arousal is often preceded by conscious or unconscious perceptions of either internal or external stimuli. Embedded memories of past events and the emotional valence attached to them influence the current perceptions of events by a process called *parataxic* distortions. Two individuals encountering the same event may experience different emotions, and may indeed react very differently because of their personal history and developmental background. Embedded and associative memories are vastly hidden from consciousness, and the emotional arousal and reactions to associated events are largely reflexive. These emotions come and go in waves in the psyche, triggered by antecedents; they are further aggravated or enhanced by the consequences of the reactions of the subject as well as the environment. Behavior-psychologists term them *antecedent, process,* and *consequents* of emotional arousal. Emotions, by definition, prompt a person to react, as well as act. However, action or reaction is neither necessary nor called for in response to an experienced emotion. Self-awareness and self-control, guided by the value systems of the individual, will determine how one controls one's reactions or actions in response to these felt emotions. One does not have to control emotions; one is called to regulate and manage their expressions. Integrated persons refuse to be controlled by their emotional arousal; they remain in charge of what they choose to do regardless of the experienced emotions. A person's happiness and success in life depend immensely on how he or she chooses to act in the context of emotional arousal. Such is termed emotional maturity. Emotional intelligence is the ability to act and respond wisely and constructively in the context of emotional arousal. Self-control and circumspection are essential ingredients of emotional intelligence. Being reflectively aware of one's emotional arousals, their nature, intensity and quality can be a highly productive pathway to self-understanding and insight into oneself.

Motivation

At the root of some of the primary emotions is motivation. A motive is a movement towards a goal; it moves or inclines us to do something to achieve an object of our desire. Motivation always represents a reason for action, whether known or unconscious. Numerous theories have been proposed to explain human motivation. While there are several ways to categorize and classify human motivation, there is general agreement that human motivations can be intrinsic or extrinsic. Intrinsic motivations are essential for survival and growth, such as the drives of hunger and thirst, self-determination, sex, the experience of competence and relatedness, and most importantly, the need to love and receive love. Many believe that religious quest for meaning is intrinsic to human motivation. Extrinsic motivations are objects, events, rewards, accomplishments, etc. that prompt us to achieve them for a value inherent in them or imposed on us by environmental forces. For example, a student may be extrinsically motivated to study hard with the hope of getting a good job; or intrinsically motivated because of the desire to know. At any rate, congruent emotions accompany motivations, the nature, and intensity of which are determined by the power of the need. Our basic needs for survival and growth take precedence over higher motives such as self-actualization. The motivation for psycho-spiritual integration is intrinsic.

Object Relations and Cognitive Triad

Of profound importance and consequence are the early representations of reality, and people in particular, in the human psyche. "Object relations" is the technical term for internal representations of people, *events, and things*. The most significant representations are the "cognitive triad" which consists of the cognitive conclusions regarding self, significant others, and life itself, especially regarding experiences of the past. These representations produce belief-systems, termed *schemata*. Such beliefs and *schemata* carry emotional overlays. These mostly unconscious processes, once formed, are tenaciously held and resistant to change, depending on the strength of their affective valence. In fact, the subsequent perceptions regarding the cognitive triad are processed to confirm and solidify these beliefs. What we already know colors what we learn anew. When new perceptions seem to contradict the tenaciously held beliefs, cognitive dissonance is produced, which in turn creates anxiety and agitation. Such tension and unrest cannot be maintained for long, urging the psyche to resolve them by either assimilating the new information in favor of the existing beliefs or occasionally accommodating by altering the current views.

Assimilation and accommodation are two crucial cognitive processes, elaborated initially by the developmental psychologist Piaget. When a new reality, object, is presented to the mind, it tries to figure out what it is and how it impacts the self and others. The mind compares the object with what it knows already through similarity or contrast and understands (assimilates) it accordingly. If the new object is unfamiliar, the person accommodates to it by accepting it as something genuinely different and thus expanding one's repertoire. In the former process, the perception is "digested," assimilated, into the existing system, while in the latter the person changes, accommodates, to the new reality.

The semi-permanent internal representations prompt a person to develop coping mechanisms. The coping mechanisms and self-adaptation are in response to the internal and external demands consciously or unconsciously experienced by the individual. It is evident that coping responses are, therefore, profoundly affected by the cognitive triad and the perception of the immediate demands of the reality. Such responses become habituated through repetition. The efficiency, utility, and productivity of these responses vary significantly depending on one's style. Now we know why two people, under the same circumstance, may process and react to the same reality very differently.

Personality

Personality is the enduring, internal, and dynamic organization of psychophysical systems within an individual, based on personal experience and the resulting stylistic adaptations of the individual (Ref. Allport, 1937.) A personality style has four core elements: experience, cognitive positions, enduring behavioral (stylistic) adjustments, and flexibility to change. Our sense of identity, the way we perceive and process internal and external reality, the manner in which we are accustomed to relating to people, events (both past, present and projected future), and our view of life itself are essential structures of personality. This personality structure and style are unique in their configurations and manifestations in each, even though we share with each other a lot of personality characteristics. All personality styles carry with them inherent strengths and liabilities. However, some personality styles are almost always problematic in any situation; these are personality disorders. The Diagnostic and Statistical Manual (DSM) defines personality disorder as follows: "A Personality Disorder is an enduring pattern of inner experience and behavior that deviates markedly from the expectations of the individual's culture, is pervasive and inflexible, has an onset in adolescence or early childhood, is stable over time, and leads to distress or impairment" (DSM-IV-TR. P.685). Examples of pathological personality styles are excessive dependence on others, false independence, oppositionality, consistent avoidance of intimacy, social interactions, etc.

Personality structure is mostly unconscious to the individual. Under ordinary circumstances, an individual does not experience conflict with his or her style. After all, he or she developed the style based on and consistent with their experience of life. This absence of conflict regarding one's style is technically termed *ego-syntonic*. When a pattern of behavior is directly challenged or creates conflicted outcomes, the person may become anxious. The mind defends such anxiety through numerous defense mechanisms. The potential awareness of something wrong with oneself is warded off to avoid stress. Psychologists have identified multiple defense mechanisms. Warding off awareness (repression) is one of the most basic and prominent. Rationalizing one's behavior, displacement of feelings, converting one emotion into another, escaping into fantasy, naïve denial of reality… etc., are examples of defensive maneuvers of the anxious mind. Despite these defense mechanisms, the repressed awareness and anxiety may still emerge creating symptoms of psychopathology. Defense mechanisms are protective and adaptive; no one entirely escapes without employing them;

however, excessive and habitual employment of such devices can seriously impair or interfere with integration.

Self-Efficacy

Among many issues related to human personality structure, perhaps, two factors are of particular importance to deserve mention here. These are self-efficacy and achievement motivation.

The scientific concept of self-efficacy was defined and studied by the social-cognitive psychologist, Albert Bandura. He defined self-efficacy as one's belief in his or her ability to complete a task and thereby achieve a specific goal. Thus self-efficacy is a cognitive stance, an attitude towards one's ability. Several research studies have been undertaken to understand the mechanism of self-efficacy, resulting in some significant findings. A person begins to develop the belief in one's ability based on four core factors of experience: personal experience of success or failure, vicarious experience or modeling (observation and imitation of others), social persuasion, and physiological factors, such as physical strength, health, etc. "Nothing succeeds like success" is derived from the common sense observation that when people succeed in something, they tend to believe they can do it again which is especially true if they attribute the success primarily to their abilities. Seeing others succeed, especially those who we believe are similar to us in ability, can have a positive impact on our self-assessment; "If she can do it, I can do it!" When there is the social reassurance to achieve, and cheer-leading, especially from those who are significant in one's life, self-efficacy increases. Finally, physiology influences self-efficacy; a person with a lot of physical stamina and good health is likely to feel more confident than a fatigued and sickly person. As is now apparent, the sense of self-efficacy can significantly affect people in what they choose as their goals and in what they decide to do.

Self-esteem is not the same as self-efficacy. Self-esteem is the result of one's evaluation of self, regarding what one would like to be, while self-efficacy is the belief in one's ability to achieve a specific goal. A person who may have high self-efficacy may or may not have high self-esteem. Competence and efficacy are assessed concerning actual results, while self-efficacy is the subjective cognition and belief related to ability. Self-efficacy does not automatically mean that the person is competent or efficacious. Self-efficacy includes the assessment of self regarding one's capacity to elicit other people's assistance to achieve the desired goal. People with high self-efficacy are often collaborators. It is interesting to note that people with high self-efficacy engage more enthusiastically in service-oriented projects and take leadership in them.

Bandura found that people with high self-efficacy tended to persevere in their efforts, while those with low self-efficacy tended to give up fast in discouragement. Psychological research indicates that it is most productive to set one's goals slightly above one's perceived ability. Such an approach leads people to broaden their experience of success. Research also has demonstrated that self-efficacy is an essential consideration in education. Good education instills greater self-efficacy in the students, propelling them to broaden their goals, deepen their habits of perseverance and hard work, and indeed giving them the experience of genuine success and achievement.

Achievement Motivation

While self-efficacy is a *belief* in one's abilities to act and achieve a result, achievement motivation is the *desire* to obtain a result. Psychologist David McClelland elaborated the theory of achievement motivation. He proposed three basic human needs in this regard, the need to achieve results primarily through one's own hard work and ingenuity, the need for power, and the need for affiliation. McClelland theorized that human beings differ in their achievement motivations based on the influence of parents, significant others, and the culture.

Human beings go through five stages of development: infancy, childhood, adolescence, adulthood, and senescence. Psychologists, especially developmental psychologists, have tried to identify the specific challenges and developmental tasks that the human being has to confront at each stage of human development. There is no disagreement that each stage of development has its unique challenges. It is important to note that failures or inadequacy in overcoming the challenges typical of each stage could have serious and deleterious consequences in the overall life-experience as well as the personality structure of a person. For example, particular experiences of failures in childhood or adolescence may continue to haunt the individual into adulthood. In fact, specific childhood traumas can trigger a post-traumatic reaction much later in adulthood.

In the context of psycho-spiritual integration, the best-fit theory of psychosocial development is, perhaps, the one elaborated by the psycho-analyst, Erik Erikson who was a second generation Freudian disciple. Erikson proposed eight distinct and identifiable stages of psychosocial development. Each stage comes with its own "crisis" and challenges. Resolving the stage-specific "crisis" is not a necessary condition to confront the demands of the next step. As life moves on, the unresolved issues continue to impact the individual's psychosocial integration adversely.

Stages of Psychosocial Development
(Adapted from Erik Erikson)

Developmental Years	Conflict	Domain
1. Infancy	trust vs. mistrust	attachment
2. Toddler	autonomy vs. shame	self-reliance
3. Early childhood	initiative vs. guilt	sense of purpose
4. Latency	industry vs. inferiority	self-efficacy
5. Adolescence	identity vs. role confusion	commitment
6. Early adulthood	intimacy vs. isolation	romantic attachments
7. Adulthood	generativity vs. stagnation	achievement
8. Late adulthood and senescence	integrity vs. despair	Evaluation of life

A child is born as entirely dependent, unable to reflect adequately and to make deliberate choices. The baby starts off with the symbiotic relationship with the mother. Separation-individuation is a process that begins when the individual confronts the fact that there are realities distinct from self. Mother is not the same as I! This produces immense, unconscious, anxiety initiating a complex of coping mechanisms. In an atmosphere of loving care, the infant is continuously soothed with nurturance and constant assurance of its safety. In normal circumstances, the helpless attachment of the child to the mother is gently and gradually weaned based on the developmental achievements of the child. So many things can potentially go wrong in this critical process of individuation-separation, especially in the early stages of development. Inadequate or deprived nurturing, premature demands on the child, overindulgence, abuse, etc., in addition to the unforeseen physical ailments and potential traumas--all these have a profound impact on the child's inner experience and resultant internal representations and attachments. These mostly unconscious representations of self, others, and the world, coupled with the hereditary and genetic makeup of the individual, form some of the foundations of our psychic structure and the basis for our styles of interpersonal relationships. Reactions and coping mechanisms develop in response to these perceptions. Psychologists postulate that the core elements of personality style start forming very early in the developmental process. However, personality structure, as a rule, is permanently solidified when the brain also stops growing between the age of twenty and twenty-four.

Developing trust in significant others and forming stable attachments are the foundational psychosocial developmental tasks of the child in the first two years of its life. The child learns early on who to trust or not. At this stage, the child develops attachments and related styles. If the child is made safe from harm, nourished and cared for consistently and predictably, it promotes healthy emotional attachments, trust, and confidence in others. Recent psychological theories and research into how children form attachments to significant others have further confirmed the importance of this process of developing trust. The existential issue of trust versus mistrust is a life-long concern; however, the foundational experience indeed starts at the very early stage of life. An essential aspect of learning that begins at this stage is becoming aware of potential dangers and learning to avoid or overcome them. Apparently, without the sense of security and certainty of ongoing nourishment and support, the capacity for discriminative assessment of persons, objects, and situations cannot be done. If one cannot identify friends, how can one know who the enemies are! As we will see later, the ability to trust significant others and life itself is an essential pre-condition for psycho-spiritual integration.

The next stage of psychosocial development is autonomy versus shame. At this time the child feels for the first time a sense that he or she can do certain things on their own. Even in their "clumsy" attempts at achieving success in simple tasks they feel a sense of accomplishment, pride, and efficacy. When such feats are encouraged, supported, and positively praised the child further develops self-confidence; however, if failure or ridicule could produce a sense of shame and poor self-worth.

When the child feels a sense of autonomy, it takes the initiative and spontaneous actions. When such effort is lacking, the child could experience a sense of guilt. A sense of guilt is different qualitatively from shame; guilt is related to a specific act or absence of required action, whereas shame is directed towards one's very being as inadequate or lacking.

Autonomy and initiative move a person to produce results and accomplishments which Erikson terms as "industry." Approximately between the ages of five to adolescent years, typically termed as latency period, productivity, mostly concerning foundational educational and physical developments, becomes the focus of psychosocial development. When "industry" is minimal, the child develops a sense of inferiority and incompetence. They may withdraw from productive activity, sometimes into a world of fantasy and imagined achievement. At this crucial period, parents and teachers play an essential role in developing solid work-habits for the child. Educators of the child need to recognize the inherent talents and gifts as well as the liabilities of the developing person. For example, if a child has dyslexia or other learning disabilities, they must be identified and circumvented.

As the young person moves on from latency to adolescence, significant physiological and psychological changes occur. Sexual maturity and corresponding hormonal changes, the sudden leap of physical stature and muscular development, etc. together with the initial and sometimes confusing feelings of attraction to others, provoke several introversive questionings of self. The questions such as "who am I? what do I want to be?" become very relevant and immediate to the adolescent. By observing self and others and their reactions, the teen begins to develop a sense of self as well as a sense of direction. The self-experimentations sometimes could take extreme forms. Adolescence is also a period observed to be a period of idealism and commitment for many. They can become very generous, adventurous, and self-giving. Very many ideals of life form at this period. Hero-worship is a consequence of such idealistic views. Adolescence is also a time when some develop a sense of religious calling involving a life of unconditional service to others.

As the person moves to young adulthood, the early experiences of sexual attractions begin to solidify into a longing for permanency and fidelity. The experience of love, especially romantic love, inherently calls for permanence, commitment, and faithfulness. Such longings traditionally end up in marriage and permanent obligations forming the basis of family life. When love is absent, thwarted or distorted, the individual is isolated emotionally with severe consequences. Such persons may develop antisocial, avoidant or schizoid personality characteristics, avoiding genuine intimacy or close relationships. Their relationship could be superficially charming, glib, avoidant, or indeed withdrawn and isolated.

The young adult settles down, usually forming a family unit. As an individual, the founding member of the new family, and an adult member of the community and society at large, his or her focus changes to actual productivity and achievement. Erikson appropriately terms the conflict of this phase as one of "generativity vs. stagnation." First of all, the demands of the family, especially those of protecting and providing for the security, comfort, and development of the children and spouse take on enormous importance. Once these are adequately secured, there are demands to be a contributing member of the community, such as one's religious institutions, charities, and other humanitarian requests. Additionally, depending on the personal needs of achievement, the person may feel compelled to strive for career achievement, literary, and political or other power-related achievements. When an individual is not generating achievements, he or she feels "stuck" or stagnated in their life. Such sense of stagnation could further erode self-efficacy, self-esteem, or even worse, a sense of failure and deep inferiority.

The final stage of psychosocial development is when the individual begins to confront the reality of mortality and the end of life. At this stage, the individual tends to look back and make assessments of life as it had been. Such evaluation of life can generate severe conflicts and feelings. The way the individual resolves the findings will have a profound impact on the experience of old age. The optimal resolution is to develop a sense of integrity with wisdom to recognize that life has been a worthwhile journey with its highs and lows, with its nights and days, and seasons. The individual learns to accept mistakes and errors as a necessary part of living. One celebrates personal achievements in the broader context of life becoming grateful for the gift and blessings of life. When a person advancing into senescence and confronting eventual death does not develop wisdom, he or she tends to become melancholic, regretful, and even despairing. It has been the broader experience of humankind that old age is a time of rejoicing in the young people in the family and loving them. At this time one may deepen one's religious sense and experience, especially if one begins to look forward to everlasting life after death. Those who believe and trust in God and an eternal life with Him after death has a better chance of achieving great peace and serenity in old age.

Psychological Programming

There is much talk that we are all "programmed" by those who are significant in our lives and the culture around us. Often this term is used pejoratively, meaning that a human being is a puppet or a computer programmed to experience life, think, feel, decide, and behave in a pre-determined manner. Such a deterministic position holds that we are essentially "conditioned" with reinforcements and we are "neuro-linguistically" programmed. B. F. Skinner, a prominent psychologist and proponent of behavioral psychology held an extreme view that we are simply a product of programming by our environment and life-circumstances. Some suggest that the way out of the programmed mind is to become critically aware of the programming and its effects in our lives. While there is some truth in the statement, the truth of the matter is that all beings are "programmed" genetically and by the environment up to an extent. Human beings are programmed to be human beings. Becoming aware of how we are programmed is very useful. However, "programming," is also an essential part of our makeup. Whether through outside influence or our own choices, we must program ourselves in most of our behavioral patterns. Such programmed behaviors are the basis of habits. Without good habits, such as learning to walk without being aware of every step or learning to read and write, we cannot function. The issue then is not about programming, but about how we program ourselves or allow ourselves to be influenced by others. The question is about the utility and value of a habitual style of being. Wisdom is in developing and maintaining good and productive habits. Just because we have been trained or taught how to be by someone else does not make it invalid or useless. Resisting appropriate formation through education is contrary to the fact of our interdependence. In our formative years, we do not have the maturity, information, and wisdom to make appropriate choices. Parents, the Church, as well as educators must make sure that the children are appropriately informed, assisted in the formation of their conscience, taught how to behave, and to have experience of faith. Part of this formation is to assist the children to become increasingly autonomous, identify their gifts, and learn to learn and make wise choices, etc. However, in the name of "avoiding external programming," we cannot allow ourselves wanton experimentation or mindless pursuits. There is value in learning from others' experience. Certain avoidable mistakes, once made, have irreversible and deleterious consequences. As we will see later, psycho-social integration requires that the individual reaches a point where self-determination is made based on deep self-awareness and personal commitment to values.

Mental Illness

A few comments on mental illness may be in order here. Mental illness is the presence of a condition that impairs and interferes with a person's cognitive processes, emotional stability, social relationships and overall, especially daily, functioning. Such dysfunctions often arise from neurological and endocrine maladies in interaction with psychological factors. Certain pathological mental conditions occur primarily from malfunctions of cognitive and emotional processes, independent of physiological origins. Pathological mental status may be produced, mostly of a temporary nature, as a result of stress-reactions to extreme environmental conditions or personal or social events, such as a catastrophe or sudden death of a significant person. Illicit drug use can cause severe mental instability as well as mimic various types of mental illnesses. Addictions to substances are physiological and psychological conditions, diseases that require both physiological and psychosocial interventions. Disorders of personality style are categorized separately from mental illnesses per se, albeit the fact that such disorders cause significant disruptions, especially in social relationships. Regardless of the etiology of these conditions, they are the source of immeasurable suffering for the subjects as well as those who relate to them. Pathological mental states have been exhaustively categorized and classified in the International Classification of Diseases (ICD) and the Diagnostic and Statistical Manual of the American Psychiatric Association (DSM). We shall not go into an elaborate discussion of the numerous categories of mental illnesses here.

Due to mental illness, a person may become incapable of processing even commonplace reality, perceiving things, persons, and events in a bizarre or distorted manner. Some of the signs of mental illness are a grandiose sense of self, such as one is God or a famous historical figure, distorted view of others as someone other than who they really are (e.g., seeing another as the "devil" or an imposter) or unrealistic interpretations of bodily sensations (e.g.. "I have undetectable germs or worms in me"), etc. Often such psychotic diseases are accompanied by severe mood disturbances, such as catatonic withdrawal, profound depression, or excessive euphoria. Emotional disturbances such as lasting depression, panic attacks, generalized anxiety, etc., are severe conditions that can affect a person's ability to function independently or productively. Certain situations can create emotional and thought imbalances, forming an acute crisis or temporary mental breakdown. Such situational reactions, if properly handled, may resolve themselves in time; however, professional help can assist the individual to manage the situation more effectively and efficiently. Crisis intervention in times of personal or communal disasters is very beneficial. Trained experts do best in assisting at times of emotional crisis arising out of disastrous events. Mental disorders can manifest as a result of known brain-disease, such as brain infection, deterioration, or intoxication or drug-withdrawal. It is vital to recognize them as such. It is important to realize that intellectual deficiency, often called mental retardation, is a condition, not a mental illness. Intellectually challenged individuals deserve to be approached without an additional label of mental illness, the same as physically challenged people are not necessarily sick. Addictions to alcohol, drugs, or other behavioral disorders are psychiatric conditions that require specialized treatment. Addictive disorders are sometimes comorbid with other mental disorders. In such cases, dual diagnoses are necessary to make their treatment more comprehensive and useful.

Individuals who have mental conditions have a much harder time achieving psycho-spiritual integration albeit the fact that many such individuals heroically achieve remarkable self-acceptance and functionality. Mentally ill individuals require compassion, support, encouragement, and psychological, medical, and spiritual care. Psycho-spiritual integration of those who are mentally sick needs separate and particular elaboration than is possible in the present discussion.

Keeping all the internal systems working together to maintain the integrity of being is the constant and ongoing task of life. An imbalance in any of the operations may profoundly affect the rest. When the systems are in proper balance, all contributing to the holistic wellbeing, we experience balance, homeostasis.

The onslaught of changes within the internal systems and the continually changing demands from the environment can threaten the homeostasis. The success of the organism to sustain homeostasis depends on the strength and inherent validity of its coping mechanisms, mostly developed through constant learning and habitual styles of coping. Integration, no matter how tenuously held, is essential to be functional. In this sense, as long as we are alive, we experience some integration. However, the quality, strength, and sustainability of integration differ within the individual as well as from individual to individual across the span of life. Discussion of integration does not necessarily focus on its mere presence, instead of on its nature, dynamics, quality, strength, and sustainability.

Psychotherapy versus spiritual direction

Before we conclude this brief synopsis of psychological foundations, it is appropriate to discuss psychotherapy as it is distinct from spiritual direction. The love-hate relationship between psychology and religion also percolated into the respective contributions of psychotherapy and spiritual guidance. Historically, psychotherapists shunned discussion of spirituality with their clients; in fact, some schools forbade the therapist to broach the subject as it would not be "scientific." Such an attitude is significantly changing; psychotherapists are now asked to take the "spirituality" of the client seriously and "utilize" them in the psychotherapeutic endeavor. The therapist is warned not to impose his or her religious or spiritual beliefs on the client. The spiritual directors, on the other hand, are quick to acknowledge the usefulness of the insights of scientific psychology. Many spiritual directors and pastoral counselors got themselves trained in psychology as well as in the art of counseling. Because of these, the boundary, as well as the distinction between psychotherapy and spiritual direction, has become blurred and sometimes confused.

The distinction between psychotherapy and spiritual guidance is valid as they refer to different processes. Psychotherapy is a healing art governed by scientific principles, monitored and licensed by legal entities as well as ethical boards of scientific disciplines. In this sense, it is very akin to medical practice. Only qualified and adequately licensed practitioners are allowed to engage in this profession. They are liable for potential malpractice lawsuits. None of these apply to spiritual direction. It is a religious endeavor and is undertaken by mutual consent between individuals. Spiritual direction is not a certified or licensed profession. In that sense anyone can volunteer, regardless of its basic ethics, to offer or receive spiritual guidance. However, in more established religions, there are presumed guidelines and ethical principles that govern spiritual direction. For example, a spiritual guide, a Guru, in Hinduism, is rarely self-assigned but recognized by the community as an experienced spiritual master who by his life, spiritual experiences, and erudition has compellingly convinced others to be capable of guiding a disciple. In Christian churches, spiritual guides are usually pastors, priests, or monastics.

More importantly, the principles, methods, procedures, and expected outcomes are very distinct between psychotherapy and spiritual direction. Of course, psychotherapy can be spiritually beneficial and spiritual. For the sake of greater clarity, the following table is provided to summarize the distinctions between the two.

As is illustrated in the Table below, the two processes are significantly different from each other. One of the remarkable issues is about the "agency"; in psychotherapy, as a rule, the relationship with the therapist is the forum for many interpretations such as interpreting the "transference neurosis" as in psychodynamic psychotherapy. In behavioral and cognitive therapies, the client depends heavily on the scientific expertise of the psychotherapist. In spiritual direction, the "director" in fact does not "direct" as a rule; he or she is an attentive witness of the spiritual movements within the client. The director clarifies through gentle and supportive inquiry how the client is interpreting and internalizing the meaning and experience of the spiritual changes.

The psychotherapist may observe that the client may need to consult a competent spiritual director to resolve spiritual and religious issues; the spiritual director may notice that psychological problems or mental illness may be significantly interfering with the spiritual experiences or interpretations of the client. On those occasions, it is wise to make the appropriate referrals. However, combining the two roles could be perilous, and may damage both processes. On occasions, either of the practitioners may successfully address a specific issue with a client.

Table 2: Major distinctions between psychotherapy and spiritual direction

	Psychotherapy	Spiritual Direction
Provider	Licensed professional	Approved by religious authority Acclaimed by the community, Ordained minister
Subject	Symptoms, mental illness Psychological problems	Religious experience, practice, spiritual issues
Method	Evidence-based scientific processes that promote change	Scripture, tradition, religious practices
Agency	Relationship with the therapist	Self, Movements of the Spirit
Outcome	Psychological Changes measurable by Tests, clinical examination.	Deeper or corrected experience of self, others, and God, Measured by self-report.

CHAPTER 3

Psychosexual Development

"As an incarnate spirit, that is a soul which expresses itself in a body and a body informed by an immortal spirit, man is called to love in his unified totality. Love includes the human body, and the body is made a sharer in spiritual love. . . Consequently, sexuality, through which man and woman give themselves to one another through the acts which are proper and exclusive to spouses, is by no means something purely biological, but concerns the innermost being of the human person as such." (See John Paul II, The Apostolic Exhortation on the Family, Familiaris Consortio, no. 11.)

In this chapter, we shall limit our discussion to the most salient aspects of psychosexual development in as much as it is relevant to psycho-spiritual integration. In modern times, the discussion of the pervasive influence of sexuality in the development and functioning of the human psyche was substantially accelerated by Sigmund Freud, the founder of Psychoanalysis, and his disciples and critics. Freud postulated five developmental stages of psychosexual growth to maturity: the oral, anal, phallic, latent, and genital stages. Freud maintained that human sexuality is an innate instinctual drive that manifests in different ways from infancy to adulthood. He also theorized, based on clinical experience, that sexuality is one of the most important drives that shape the entire personality and mental function of an individual. Many of his critics vehemently objected to several of his theoretical proposals, particularly his "pansexual" interpretations of psychodynamics. Consistent with the modern approach of empirical sciences that generally shuns teleological ("final cause") analysis, Freud concentrated on the pervasive influence of sexuality in all phases of human development. He was averse to spiritualize any aspect of sexuality; instead, he focused more on the experiential and dynamic aspects of the human sexual drive. He regarded voluntary abstinence from genital expressions of sexuality as a defensive maneuver to ward off anxiety and guilt arising out of the so-called Oedipal Complex. He named this defense "sublimation," mostly an intellectual and reactive process. Regardless of the merits of his analysis, Freud's most significant contribution in this regard, perhaps, was the fact that he made psychosexual development an essential and open topic of scientific discourse in psychology.

Sexual development moves from auto-eroticism to other-directed sexual attraction, and finally to sexual intimacy with another. This innate and powerful drive seeks to preserve the species, through the establishment of families and generation of progenies. Nature has attached highly self-reinforcing tension-reduction--which one experiences as pleasure--to sexual activity. While human beings share with the rest of the mammals the biological mechanisms of sexuality, human sexuality takes on qualitatively different meanings as well as expressions. Because of self-reflective intelligence and freedom of choice, the manifestation of this natural drive can and does vary in individuals. Precisely because of this, and because of its great significance for the human society, the expression and social exercise of sexuality has been regulated and institutionalized in all human communities. The biological and social sciences, specifically, developmental psychology, have demythologized human sexuality. This demythologization process has been partly responsible for the "sexual revolution" witnessed in the latter half of the 20th century. Suffice it to say, severe challenges to the traditional notions of sexual expression are being raised, causing considerable destabilization in moral, cultural, and religious institutions related to human sexuality. Prominent examples are the partially successful normalization of homosexuality, single parenthood, pre-marital sexual union, etc.

The psychological experience of human sexuality almost always is associated with the emotion of love. The complexity of defining and describing the emotion of love, from a psychological perspective, is obvious. Developmental psychology starts the discussion of love with primary narcissism. Primary narcissism is essentially the drive towards self- preservation, nourishment, and enhancement of pleasure. As the child individuates, the reality principle makes it aware of the existence of others. The internal representations of these "objects" are cathected with emotional overtones including the feeling of love towards them. The "good objects" are loved and the "bad objects" are hated or repulsed. Sometimes the same object is "split" into good and bad, creating corresponding responses of love and hatred towards the same object, depending on which split-part is engaged by the mind in a given situation. As the person matures, the good and bad aspects of the objects are integrated into a realistic whole. The primary self-love matures into legitimate self-interest and love for oneself which psychoanalysts term as secondary narcissism. However, an individual who becomes fixated and totally preoccupied with oneself demonstrates a pathological condition, called narcissistic personality disorder. Such a person has inherent difficulty to empathize with others, often manifesting an empty grandiosity, entitlement, and self-importance. As the person physically and psychologically develops, erotic attractions are experienced towards others. Erotic attractions to persons of the same sex are generally suppressed depending on the specific dynamics present in the socialization process. This issue is highly controverted in modern society. Four decades ago, homosexual attractions were considered a pathological fixation at this developmental stage. The American Psychiatric Association has removed the pathological label attached to homosexual attractions asserting that homosexual attractions and choices do not necessarily suggest psychopathology. Regardless of this controversy or its current settlement as "normal", the majority of the population moves on to heterosexual attractions. A romantic attraction that is pervasive and preoccupying in a person's psyche is called "falling in love". Falling in love is a natural phenomenon and is not necessarily a chosen emotion. Depending on the availability of the object of love and his or her response, this romantic emotion may mature into a relationship of mutual love and may ultimately move into a permanent relationship in marriage. Cultural situations vary in the manner in which this phenomenon manifests itself. For example, "falling in love" may develop after the marriage, such as in an arranged marriage. It is also possible that a couple who have entered into an arranged marriage, may choose to love each other as sexually intimate and permanent partners in life without ever "falling in love", suggesting the fact that for a successful marriage, what is necessary is love, not necessarily the experience of having "fallen in love".

A careful examination of the process of romantic love seems to suggest a movement from primary narcissism to loving another person for the sake of love itself. Traditionally, some writers have described it as three movements: narcissism, erotic love, and agape. Agape is the culmination of the evolution of love when a person gifts himself or herself entirely and unconditionally for the beloved. Sexual intimacy at the agape level is considered psychologically and spiritually the most fulfilling. The mutual and selfless love of the couple generates new life, directing the couple to care for their children with devotion and dedication.

St. John Paul II in his celebrated instructions on the "theology of the human body" has been the most explicit in clarifying the meaning and significance of the human body. The human body is the sacramental expression of the human spirit and cannot be viewed independently of the human person. The human body is not an appendage to the soul, shed and gotten rid of at the time of death. It is a principle of human being and integral expression and visibility of the human spirit. The human soul does not *have* a body; it manifests itself as one with the body without which one cannot be a human being. There is no duality here; only integral unity of being. When we touch the human body, we are contacting the human person, whose dignity resides in his or her immortal image of God.

> *"In fact, man is called to love as an incarnate spirit, that is, soul and body in the unity of the person. Human love hence embraces the body, and the body also expresses spiritual love . . . realized in a truly human way only if it is an integral part of the love by which a man and a woman commit themselves totally to one another until death" (Familiaris Consortio, no. 11).*

Sexuality is, therefore, the manifestation of the human spirit more than a mere physical and instinctual drive. Without the spirit, human sexuality is reduced to a drive akin to those of the animals.

The Christian approach to human sexuality has centered around two essential themes: first, the God-given ability to exercise sexuality for the sustenance of the intimate relationship and bond of the married couple and the generation of children and cementing of the integrity of the family; second, the deliberate choice to deny oneself the genital expression of sexuality for the sake of the Kingdom of God. Both affirm the high value of the gift of sexuality. The Christian perspective elevates the mere biological mechanisms and psychological attractions to a more profound and particular expression of love and self-giving. Therefore, the Christian understanding of sexuality is that it is an interpersonal phenomenon. Rooted in the person, it naturally is directing the person to another, necessitating its meaningful fulfillment only in authentic self-gift to each other. The sublime view of sexuality within the context of marriage is declared by the Scripture to be sacramental, representing the mystery of Christ's love for the Church.

> *"This is a great mystery, and I mean in reference to Christ and the Church; however, let each one of you love his wife as himself and let the wife see that she respects her husband" (Eph. 5:32).*

Therefore, the Christian understanding of sexual maturity and integration is rooted in the spiritual experience of Christ's love for His Church. Christ is the Logos of God, the total self-gift of the Father, for us, for whom He gave up His life, which we now have by grafting on to Him. The sexual union between husband and wife is the most intimate and sacramental expression of Christian love, except the spiritual and close relationship with God through grace (See Gaudium et Spes no.48). Love culminates in agape, the total gift of oneself to the beloved. Consecrated celibacy also is expected to be at the agape level; it is a direct expression of intimate imitation of Christ, and a sign to the world that the intimacy of marriage is pointing towards the ultimate intimacy with God. The consecrated celibate follows Christ, who gave himself entirely and without reservation to all humankind in the service of God's Kingdom.

> "Christ proposes the evangelical counsels, in their great variety, to every disciple…"The state of consecrated life is thus one way of experiencing a "more intimate" consecration, rooted in Baptism and dedicated totally to God… In the consecrated life, Christ's faithful, moved by the Holy Spirit, propose to follow Christ more nearly, to give themselves to God who is loved above all and, pursuing the perfection of charity in the service of the Kingdom, to signify and proclaim in the Church the glory of the world to come." (Catechism of the Catholic Church #915-916)

Married life and consecrated celibate life are both, have to be, legitimate and sublime expression of human sexuality.

When human sexuality is detached from its spiritual underpinnings, it leads to apparent deviations both psychological and spiritual. From a psychological point of view, fixations at the autoerotic or erotic stage (using another for one's pleasure) prevent a person from experiencing the mature expression and meaning of human sexuality. From a spiritual point of view, using one's and others' body as objects of pleasure or mere self-satisfaction become an offense against one's dignity and a violation of nature's purposes, thereby rendering it as an offense against the Creator himself. Jesus has taken it to the most intimate psychological level; even deliberate entertaining ("looking") of a naturally occurring sexual desire for another is tantamount to infidelity.

> "But I say to you that everyone who looks at a woman lustfully has already committed adultery with her in his heart" (Mt 5:28).

A consistent awareness of the sacredness and meaning of human sexuality and a commitment to conform one's behavior accordingly is the necessary state of a sexually integrated Christian.

The question is whether a deliberately chosen abstinence from sexual intimacy is healthy. Deliberate suppression of the naturally given sexuality or its unconscious repression has its psychological consequences depending on the situation. Sexuality in normal circumstances demands expression within the confines of socialization. Neurotic symptoms emerge when sexuality is suppressed, and much worse, repressed for defensive purposes by the unconscious. The psychoanalytic view of the defense of sublimation is that it is an unconscious process. However, a conscious redirecting of sexual energy is not only possible but has been demonstrated to be capable of enhancing the quality of life. We may call it conscious and deliberate Sublimation which is a process of redirecting the instinctual energy consciously for a higher purpose. Thus, there are only two ways of exercising sexuality without doing damage to the human psyche: a legitimate expression of sexuality or its conscious sublimation for a higher purpose. The celibate life deliberately chosen in consecrated life is a legitimate sublimation of the sexual instinct to exercise Christian charity in a freer and universal manner. Secondly, as was discussed earlier, celibacy is consciously adopted as an intimate expression of one's imitation of Christ and for the sake of His Kingdom, and as a visible eschatological witness to the world. In this instance sexuality is not suppressed or repressed; its powerful energy is redirected for a higher and noble purpose.

It is necessary to practice deliberately and mindfully appropriate containment, expression, and abstinence of the sexual drive. Failures in this regard can and do occur. However, success in achieving integration is demonstrably possible with the grace of God. The struggles in different states of life are different and specific to those states. Self-control is an essential ingredient of purity of heart; it controls one's desires and passions instead of the emotions and passions controlling the person. A conscious sublimation of sexuality cannot be practiced productively without prayer and establishment of loving relationships in the context of selfless service. It is interesting to note that those who exercise self-control become free to be spontaneous and loving, thereby experiencing life in its real depth. For example, happily married couple and dedicated celibates are free to develop intimate friendships without the undue interference of sexual pre-occupation or worry.

CHAPTER 4

Foundations of Christian spirituality

Personal encounter in the faith of the risen Lord Jesus Christ is the foundation of Christian spirituality. Actively and willingly accepting Jesus Christ as one's savior, God, and Lord of one's life is the commitment of faith the Christian makes. This faith-commitment implies several foundational facts and beliefs.

1. Human beings are destined for everlasting communion with the triune God, Father, Son, and the Holy Spirit. Without God's initiative, salvific grace, and pure gift of redemption, no human being can achieve this end through his or her effort, no matter how heroic. The Good News, the Gospel, is that God has accomplished this definitively in Jesus Christ who is the incarnate Word of God, truly God and man. In uniting oneself with His life, suffering, death, and resurrection, a person attains his God-appointed destiny, the blissful and everlasting union with God.

2. While the infinite love of God offers redemption and the possibility of salvation to us, He cannot save us without our accepting His loving invitation and Grace. The definitive sign of our acceptance of God's love is our conformity to His will in our life.

3. The forces of evil, our natural inclinations to be self-centered, and the ungodly tendencies that are prevalent in the world tend to tempt us often. No one escapes failures in this regard. Sin is our constant companion during our earthly existence, even when we set our eyes firmly on God's will. However, where sin has abounded, Grace has abounded even more for those who seek God's will. With God's grace and our cooperation with His grace, we can overcome evil.

4. The Spirit of God comes to our aid continuously, praying deep within us, as we yearn for protection from every sort of evil, including our sinful tendencies. A Christian is called for continuous conversion-turning around and towards God-to an infinitely patient, long-suffering, and all-loving God. God invites us to communicate with Him regularly through prayer and contemplation of His Word in the sacred Scriptures, the double-edged sword that encourages, corrects, and instructs us in the ways of God. As long as we are alive on this earth, we have the opportunity to turn to and be accepted by God's redemptive love.

5. To aid us in our daily struggles and weakness, Jesus makes Himself present through His Church, His sacramental presence in the world. Through the sacraments offered through the Church, we are incorporated into His mystical body, like the branches of the vine, allowing the sap of life to flow into us. Jesus makes Himself present to us on every occasion of our life. In Baptism we are cleansed of all our sins; we are reborn in Him. We are confirmed and strengthened by His Holy Spirit in the anointing of Confirmation. When we repent of our sins, He forgives us time and again through the sacrament of reconciliation. He nourishes us with His body and blood through the Eucharist which also unites us with His community of believers, the mystical body of Christ, the Church. He blesses couples at their marriage and building of the family. He provides us with His priests, who are given the authority to forgive our sins in His name, and consecrate our gifts of bread and wine into His very body and blood, the source of our spiritual nourishment. Finally, at the time of illness or the point of death, He is there anointing us again, assuring of His presence and everlasting love.

6. The Scriptures instruct us that our salvation is not merely an individual event. Redemption occurs in the context of the community of believers, indeed in the context of the entire humanity and creation. Without an active and loving relationship with other human beings, one cannot authentically experience and relate to God's love.

"He who says he is in the light and hates his brother is in the darkness still. He who loves his brother abides in the light," (1Jn 1:9, 10)

We are asked to pray that God forgives us as we forgive our brothers and sisters. In as much as a person is willing to love and serve others, the Lordship of Jesus in one's life becomes real. Without loving and serving others, we cannot reach Jesus. His commandment to those who choose to follow Him is unambiguous:

"By this, all men will know that you are my disciples if you have the love for one another" (Jn13:35).

Our final judgment depends on how we served others during our lifetime, especially those who were in genuine need of our assistance (Mt.26). God demands that we worship Him together with others. Even as we isolate ourselves physically from others for the quiet of personal prayer, we carry our brothers and sisters with us before God.

CHAPTER 5

Essential pre-requisites for psycho-spiritual integration

From a Catholic Christian perspective, the psycho-spiritual integrative process happens best in the context of several pre-conditions.

1. An attitude of continuous conversion towards what is good

The bulk of humanity has always held that human beings are morally responsible for their actions, thereby asserting the existence of freedom of choice. This position holds that deliberate actions with functional knowledge of the nature of the situation is typically a human act and therefore, are imputable. In short, deliberate perpetration of evil behavior is inexcusable, immoral, and therefore, sinful. It is an act that alienates one from oneself, others, and God. Psycho-spiritual integration is not possible if a person maintains a deliberate intention to live a life of evil. Deliberate evil is the antithesis of a psychologically and spiritually integrated life. In other words, psycho-spiritual integration is relevant only if one has at least the inherent goodwill of being disposed towards good. A willingness to turn away from what is evil and a desire to turn towards what is right is the foundational precondition for psycho-spiritual integration.

2. A disposition to be mindful and self-reflective

Human beings are distinct from other animals in their capacity to be self-aware and self- reflective. This ability to view oneself as an object of awareness, to observe oneself standing "outside oneself," is the remarkable ability that produces artistic creation, civilizations, and moral qualities. In fact, this ability is the foundation of psychological and spiritual development and growth. However, this self-reflective ability is not always utilized consciously, creating a life of automatic and commonplace reactions and responses. Such people are moved by and at the mercy of their impulses and the impact of their environment. They float like a leaf in the current, letting the currents take them to whatever shore they would reach; they are not the captains of their ships not having deliberated and made a careful decision on their courses or their outcomes. Hence the adage: a life without reflection is not worth living. Willingness and a deliberate choice to be aware and reflective of self is the second essential precondition for psycho-spiritual integration.

3. Self-awareness and a willingness to be open

Self-awareness requires an openness of heart and mind. Unfortunately, many human beings, often unconsciously, block awareness, both of themselves and their surroundings. Four-fifths of human consciousness is blocked by mental defenses to ward off anxiety stemming from a variety of seemingly threatening internal and external sources. Depth psychology has contributed substantially to illustrate this inner resistance to self-awareness and mindfulness. Early on in our development, we learn that awareness of certain aspects of our life could be painful and be threatening to our very existence. Therefore, it becomes adaptive to soothe ourselves by blocking the recognition of certain aspects of our psyche. While such defensive maneuvers of the mind can be protective, this burying-the-head-in-the-sand approach can prevent us from dealing effectively and creatively with the essential existential and practical aspects of life. Many of the mental illnesses have at their root this suppressive dynamics. The unconscious can interfere with the Integration of personality and spirituality. To be aware that we may not be aware, a willingness to confront this lack of awareness and to have the courage and wisdom to improve one's perception is the third precondition for psycho-spiritual integration. Without relaxed openness and knowledge, it is not possible to integrate life successfully.

4. Freedom from excessive anxiety and fear

Fear and anxiety are considerable obstacles to psycho-spiritual integration. All human beings are subject to the plague of fear and anxiety.

When these reach excessive levels, the person is paralyzed, confining him or her often to their nearest safety-nets such as the home. We experience fear when we perceive an object that is threatening to our wellbeing. On the other hand, anxiety is fear without a specific object. It is an extremely uncomfortable feeling of impending doom of some sort, without knowing what is threatening us. It agitates the person to the core of his or her being. The resultant flight-or-fight reaction produces both physiological and psychological discomfort. Since the object is not specific, the anxious person tries to escape without remedy. Removing excessive fear and anxiety is an essential precondition for psycho-spiritual integration.

5. Freedom from Skepticism, Agnosticism, and Atheism

Not knowing is not the same as doubting. It is a truism to state that no human can know everything. Acceptance of not-knowing can lead to openness to the mysteries of reality, especially the ever transcendent aspects of it. However, not knowing can also lead one to debilitating skepticism and doubt. The skeptic soothes himself by concluding falsely that one should stay focused on what one knows and not bother with what is beyond his ken. This appears benign at first sight; however, paradoxically the skeptic, sometimes without awareness, is undermining as well as doubting the truth of what he or she "knows" by denying the truth of what transcend his or her understanding. Ultimately, the skeptic is intellectually and spiritually paralyzed in the marsh-land of the concrete. Agnosticism is an obvious progeny of radical skepticism. The agnostic can appear resolute in his resentment of his limitations. He throws the baby with the bath water and sometimes even ridicules those who see the value of the certainty of transcendent aspects of reality which is called faith. The fact is that there is no escape from faith; even those who claim that they have no faith have indirectly asserted a faith that life can be meaningful without faith, which is not a provable assertion. All perceptions and thoughts require a ground—a horizon—or a "background" as the Gestalt-psychologists call it; faith is directed towards the necessary and absolute horizon and ground of all relative and finite realities. A healthy skepticism about assertions of others is not what is called into question. Denying the foundational truth of what stands beyond the knowledge of a limited mind is the bane of the confirmed skeptic and agnostic. This blocks openness, inquiry, and deliberate and committed search. Science, for example, by definition is skeptical- it ought to be so- but science knows, acknowledges, and assiduously searches for what is not known, with the certainty that there are more to be known. Science may question the validity of its inferences without being skeptical of proven facts, as well as the distinct possibility of discovering yet unknown facts. The skeptic on the other hand is closed and makes no search. Skepticism and agnosticism are serious hindrance to psycho-spiritual integration. Openness to the mystery of life and faith--the inner assurance and proof of what is not known--is another essential precondition of psycho-spiritual integration.

It is said that atheism is the early state of a reflective person. When one looks at the vastness of the Universe and its enormous and inscrutable mysteries, one could feel overwhelmed. It is unfathomable to postulate that one being could be the source of it all, both of the order and chaos. An anthropomorphic presentation of a creator and provider of this universe may appear to insult the intelligence of an inquiring man. In that sense a false God is worse than no God. Precisely because of this, sages throughout human history have postulated and formulated an absolute being largely in negation-terms, mostly in terms of transience and complexity. The atheist in rejecting anthropomorphism because of his overwhelming reaction to the enormity and vastness of the Universe is unwittingly being anthropomorphic himself! He illogically thinks that because it is incomprehensible for us to conceive how one being can be in charge of such humanly incomprehensible enormity, such a being does not exist. He misses the meaning of the aphorism: "Not to be encompassed by the greatest, but let oneself be encompassed by the smallest—such is divine" (Holderlin). God is neither overwhelmed by the so-called enormity nor by infinitesimal smallness; we are! Absolute being, by the very nature, stands beyond the conceptions of a relative mind. "Big and small" are human terms confined to space and time; God is not bound by either. To paraphrase G.K. Chesterton, God loves His "little universe"! You cannot hold the ocean in a small cup. The incomprehensibility of the infinite and absolute nature of God does not suggest His non-existence. The existence of an absolute being is an intellectual and spiritual necessity for the relative mind. However, frustrated by the incomprehensibility of the transcendent absolute, the atheist also throws the baby with the bath water. Unlike the skeptic or agnostic the atheist may be honestly rejecting the false postulations of God. But he goes too far and deprives himself of the essential relationship with the transcendent. Without the absolute in his life, he languishes in the valley of existential futility. From a Christian point of view, it is impossible to achieve psycho-spiritual integration without God in one's life.

6. Freedom from fanaticism, fundamentalism, and dogmatism

At the opposite extreme of atheism is a conscious or unconscious setting aside or outright rejection of human reason. Fanaticism, dogmatism, and fundamentalism are the nefarious opposites of unbelief. Genuine faith reaches out to the reason for satisfying the fundamental need of the intellect to know. The human understanding and reason must be at the service of faith. An intelligent person acknowledges the mysteries of life and reality. The rationality and intellect are made peaceful in the humble and loving contemplation of the questions they raise. We assimilate the mystery of life asymptotically. While it always stands beyond the full comprehension of the intellect, a mystery unfolds layers of its depth, satisfying the contemplator unendingly. It humbles us while beckoning us to ever new depths of understanding and centering. Starting with the Gospel of John, the noblest aspect of human insights, gained through philosophical reasoning, was integrated into faith-formulations. Throughout the centuries human philosophy and thinking have contributed substantially to our understanding of God's revelation in Jesus Christ. Rejection of human reason will deteriorate our contemplation into mere pietistic traditions and rituals. As Tertullian stated, Christ is the Truth, not custom. The truth is, by definition, intelligible and open to reason, though not contained by it.

Dogmas, by definition, are formulations of mysteries, not grounds for fanatical and fixated interpretation. Our understanding and penetration of the creeds are always growing in depth. The fault is not with the dogmas; the problem is with our penetration of them. Fundamental doctrines of faith are often formulated as negating our limitations of comprehension while affirming a reality that is transcendent. Humble and relaxed contemplation of dogmas produces openness and serenity; on the other hand, dogmatism is the arrogant assumption that one has understood the mystery.

> There is an organic connection between our spiritual life and the dogmas. Dogmas are lights along the path of faith. They illuminate it and make it secure. Conversely, if our life is upright, our intellect and heart will be open to welcome the light shed by the dogmas of faith. (Catechism of the Catholic Church: 89)

Fundamentalism is a puerile and servile progeny of hidden dogmatism. Dogmatism and fundamentalism are premature fixations of the mind that presumes full understanding. In such attitudes, there is neither the openness to the mystery nor the humility in one's intellectual limitations. Fundamentalism arrogates that human language can capture the mystery fully; it is the antithesis of genuine faith in a living God. The tragedy of fundamentalists is that they sincerely believe they are loyal to the Word of God while they fail to appreciate that God has spoken through the limited language of man. Just because God has pitched His tent in our midst, we should not presume that the tent can fully contain Him; because God's Word adopts the human language, we should not assume that human language can adequately express Him. Just because God is truly present in the scriptures, we cannot assert that He is only there. Of course, the Word of God is absolute and inerrant; but our understanding of it shall always fall short. This humility is lacking sorely in the fundamentalist, despite his or her protestations that they are loyal to God's Word.

Fanaticism is another form of fundamentalism, a more deadly cousin. The fanatics have concluded that they have the truth in fullness and anyone who does not accept their positions is an enemy of God, a heathen, an unbeliever. Fanaticism is, in fact, a psychological defense against genuine love. Fanaticism is the hidden face of extreme hate fueled by narcissism. The murderous rage of the fanatic has caused immense havoc not only in human endeavor but also in creating a false and antagonistic view of religion in reasonable minds. By their very nature, fanaticism, dogmatism, and fundamentalism militate against true psycho-spiritual integration. Freedom from this type of deleterious attitudes is a significant and essential precondition to functional integration.

7. Freedom from superstition.

Superstition is a false and unproven association of events with one's belief. Superstition, while a conditioned response, is also a psychological defense against anxiety. The superstitious mind clutches on straws to explain phenomena and generalizes, and often a faith statement out of it. Faith and superstition have the common element of intransigence because superstition mimics belief and arrogates unto itself faith's properties. That is why there is no easy way out of a well-established superstition. Going contrary to an entrenched notion causes significant anxiety, leading to controlling behavior such as obsessions or compulsions. Superstitions may generate ritualistic and compulsive behaviors; this could mimic genuine prayer or symbolic expressions of worship. Such ritualistic performance falsely comforts the performer but does not truly enhance or improve the quality or depth of life.

> *What to me is the multitude of your sacrifices? Says the Lord; I have had enough of burnt offerings of rams and the fat of fed beasts; I do not delight in the blood of bulls, or of lambs, or of he-goats... Bring no more vain offerings; incense is an abomination to me. New moon and Sabbath and the calling of assemblies—I cannot endure iniquity...cease to do evil, learn to do good; seek justice, correct oppression; defend the fatherless, plead for the widow (Is 1:13-17; also see Heb 10: 5-7)*

Human history indicates the tendency of the human mind to mythologize the Universe and human experiences.

> *"Claiming to be wise, they became fools, and exchanged the glory of the immortal God for images resembling mortal man and birds and animals and creeping things." (Rom 1:22-23).*

Christian faith demythologized the superstitions and replaced them with the Truth of the living God. However, the history of the Church demonstrates that we have a continuing tendency to replace the sound practice of justice and love with superstitious beliefs and practices. Rituals of worship and religious expressions are beneficial only in the context of genuine faith and corresponding practice.

8. Freedom from self-righteousness and self-sufficiency

The reign of God belongs to those poor in spirit. Self-sufficiency and self-righteousness are severe obstacles to spiritual integration. A self-righteous person demonstrates an entitled position which is in psychological terms, self-centered and narcissistic, a defense against being aware of one's failures and unworthiness, cultivated through a false conviction of the merits of one's actions, a compulsive conformity that enslaves the soul in the most subtle form. Such an attitude sets aside the truth of our lives, that everyone has fallen short of the glory of God and that at the end of the day, we are just worthless servants (Rom 3: 10-17). "If we say we have no sin, we deceive ourselves, and the truth is not in us" (Jn 1:8). We build in vain, without the Builder holding us up. A prerequisite for psycho-spiritual integration from the Christian perspective is the recognition that no one is righteous except for God's grace of justification. No man is an island. As related beings, we need to recognize our interdependence on each other and total dependence on God. Loving union with The Other is our ultimate psychological and spiritual goal. We indeed are *beings-for.* Self-sufficiency and self-righteousness militate against this goal.

9. Humility and willingness to correct oneself.

Humility is first of all the awareness and acceptance of the fact of our total dependence on God for our being and sustenance. Secondly, it means that we are in fact sinners and have fallen short; and we need to be willing to correct the error of our ways continuously. Thirdly, we indeed depend on each other in coming to know ourselves; feedback from others is necessary for our development and well-being. However, an unwillingness to admit our defects, mistakes, and more importantly our serious wrongdoings, and a lack of awareness of the sources of these errors, could severely hinder our effort at integration. Human greatness is directly proportional to the manner in which one can overcome one's failures with God's and other's help.

10. Live in the present, mindful of the past and hopeful of the future

It is trite to say that we live in the dimensions of time and space. In many ways our past influences the present, and both shape our future. However, those of us who neglect the present with the preoccupations of the past or future are missing life, as it unfolds here and now. Life is truly in the present; past is a memory, and the future is only a hope. However, the truth is that the meaning of the memory and the hope for the future depend on how we attend to the present. Psycho-spiritual integration always happens in the present. Impermanence is the essential nature of time, and we are creatures swimming in this ever-changing ocean. Integration, therefore, is not a static reality but an ongoing process in time and space. Those who believe that they have arrived have missed the boat; those who think that they will arrive only later are also not in the boat. The Kingdom of God is upon us. *Now* is the time to open the door. "Behold I stand at the door and knock..." (Rev 3:20). Those who neglect the present moment burying themselves in memory or the future do not achieve integration.

11. Trusting in life

A fundamental assumption in psycho-spiritual integration is to know that life is in our favor and on our side. Many of us live our lives fearful of impending doom, worrying that something or other will pounce on us from the hidden bushes. An attitude that life is not on our side and that we must fend for ourselves against life itself is a severe hindrance to psycho-spiritual integration. Worry is an enemy of peace. It is true that we live in the "valley of tears." However, it is also true that God is our shepherd, who guides us through the valley of darkness. Inner assurance that everything will work out for good for those whom God loves is an essential prerequisite for integrating life. God loves every living being and cares for us beyond our expectations, and therefore, we should not worry.

Therefore do not be anxious, saying, 'What shall we eat?' or 'What shall we drink?' or 'What shall we wear?' For the Gentiles seek after all these things, and your heavenly Father knows that you need them all. (Mt 6: 31, 32).

12. Accepting Jesus Christ as the Lord

In Jesus God has overcome evil, including death, and has affirmed all that is good. God has gifted us with spiritual freedom and salvation. From a Christian perspective, it is essential that we actively accept the Good News in Jesus Christ, Our Lord. We rejoice in this affirmation and knowledge. Christian spirituality is not a religion; it is the fulfillment by God of all religious quest and earnings. He has not come to abolish the Law, but to fulfill it. The futile search of man for God has been made fruitful by the search for man by God. He has come down to us and dwelt among us, not because of our goodness, prayers, or sacrifices; He has pitched His tent in our midst because He loved us even as we betray Him. God loved us first. Our love is a free response and consequence of God's love. God, for us, is not just the transcendent almighty beyond our reach, He has become one of us; He walks with us and shares our life. Accepting Jesus as our Lord and Savior is the most significant positive step a person can take towards the integration of his or her being. Psycho-spiritual integration is impossible for a Christian without a personal relationship with the Lord Jesus Christ. We must be grafted on to him as the branches of the vine; otherwise, we have no life.

"And this is the testimony that God gave us eternal life, and this life is in his Son" (1Jn4: 11).

13. Integrating spirituality with religious faith

There is much talk about distinguishing religion from spirituality. This ous distinction is spurious and without merit. Religion is the quest of man for meaning and God. Christian faith is the active acceptance of God's revelation of Himself. Christian spirituality is the development of the personal experience of the pure gift of God's revelation in Jesus Christ and our response to Him. Therefore, spirituality is born of genuine religion, as a child from the mother. Those who insist that it is not necessary to be religious to be spiritual are in fact declaring that they do not need a mother to be born, or much less to be brought up. Such confusion is maintained by identifying spiritual life with sterile forms of "religiosity" and "rituals." It is possible, and indeed it happens often sadly, that one can seek refuge in traditional practices and rituals without love and for the sake of it. Such emptiness is neither religion nor spirituality; they are deviations and indeed become superstitious behaviors. It is neither fair nor truthful to pitch empty religious practices against authentic and meaningful religious experiences. Religion is at its best when it generates genuine spiritual integration. Religion and spirituality are not antithetical to each other. Indeed from a Christian point of view, there is no authentic spirituality unguided by the living Body of Christ, the Church, through its mystery-celebrations and the contemplation of God's Word.

14. Discernment of the Spirits

The human psyche is the conscious locus of interaction between God and man. However, the human psyche is also the locus of the interaction of other Spirits. Apart from the human spirit itself, we are engaged by the Spirit of God as well as His messenger spirits. Additionally, we have to be wary and aware of the activities of the evil Spirit which is separate and real, often tangibly manifested in the "spirit of the world." The human psyche is, therefore, a battlefield of Spirits. It is vital that we become adept, with the help of God, in discerning the Spirits that try to influence our lives. While these movements may be loud and persuasive, as free beings, we are ultimately responsible for our decisions and actions. No Spirit can force us to act against our free will. Even God cannot violate His irretrievable gift of free choice. Awareness of the Spirits at work and a cautious attitude to discern them is an essential prerequisite for spiritual and psychological integration. Neither the virtuous nor the sinful are exempt from these influences. Under certain complicated circumstances of life, it is easier to do what is right than to know what is right. The endeavor to integrate one's life is hardly possible outside the guidance of the Word of God, the teachings of the Church, and the competent instructions of a spiritual companion.

Even the most sincere could be deceived into the mire of confusion and despair without discernment of the Spirits. (See the Chapter below on the Discernment of Spirits)

15. A life of authentic prayer, guided by the Word of God

According to St. Thomas Aquinas, prayer is "an expression of man's desire for God", an inherent need of the *Homo Religiosus*. Prayer, as Jesus himself showed by his example of intimate communion with the Father, is essential for spiritual as well as psychological integration. However this spontaneous need to pray needs training and cultivation. The disciples asked Jesus to teach them how to pray (Lk.11: 1). Prayer, be it contemplation, meditation, or attentive reading of the Word of God…, is a double-edged sword. This prerequisite for spiritual life is at once potentially dangerous as it is essential. Prayer is our attempt at direct communion with God. As the scripture tells us, genuine prayer is prompted and guided by the Spirit of God (Rom 8:26). However, prayer is also a human act. The primary effect of prayer is that we dispose ourselves to be transformed by God's love, experience his infinite patience and forgiveness… and most importantly we are made ready to conform to His will for us. This requires silencing of our mind so that in the stillness we can listen to God. However, often in our chatter we end up looking to ourselves and mistake our self-promptings for God's voice. Prayer then becomes a self-fulfilling prophecy, confirming our will as if it were from God. This is a dangerous situation. The classical example given in the scripture is the prayer of the self-righteous Pharisee who went away self-satisfied but not justified by God; whereas the repentant publican, who did not dare to enter the house of God, went away with the blessing of God. Prayer can be used to rationalize and even block God's inspirations. False revelations are plentiful in pseudo-mystical prayer as we learn from history. While prayer is an essential means of psycho-spiritual integration, one should enter into it with great care and proper disposition. Self-righteous and self-centered prayer can mislead the intelligent as well as the imbecile. While without a life of constant prayer, spiritual integration is impossible; improper exercise of prayer can lead to deceit and disintegration.

CHAPTER 6

Essential Elements of Psycho-spiritual Integration

It is easier to define psychopathology and mental illness than psychological health. It is equally valid that we can spot more easily a sinful existence than a holy one. Because of this, some define mental well- being as an absence of mental illness; and falsely define spiritual integration as the mere absence of active sinfulness. Unfortunately, such an approach does not address how well a person is psychologically or spiritually integrated. For our purposes, we need to elaborate on those essential elements of psychological and spiritual integration. Six factors stand out, albeit not exhaustively, in this regard: mindfulness, authenticity, spontaneity, intimacy, autonomy, and openness. In the future discussion, we shall incorporate the psychological and spiritual principles associated with these essential integrative processes and qualities.

Mindfulness

Mindfulness is the awareness of self, others, and life, focusing primarily on the present, one's thoughts, feelings, and sensations in a relaxed and accepting state of mind. It is an active and deliberate decision to pay attention without compulsion or obsession. In mindfulness, awareness is allowed to develop without the dampening effect of immediate value-judgment of the content. In this type of attentiveness, one employs emotional detachment. As if standing outside of oneself, one chooses to observe what is happening inside and outside the self actively. A mindful person does not tell himself: "I shouldn't feel or think this or that way." Instead, he or she says: "Let me be aware of how I think, feel, and react while I remain in control of what I decide to do." A mindful person is not interested in "controlling" his/her natural emotions, instead of regulating their flow and controlling his/her expressions and actions. Thoughts and feelings are allowed to come and go as a person watches the waves of an ocean come and go at the whim of the wind. Mindfulness assists a person to set aside deliberately, if necessary, an unwanted or overly intrusive feeling; this is done in relaxation and with awareness. However, mindfulness does not relinquish autonomy, the ability to choose and initiate action or response. The mindful person is in control of what he or she does. Emotions are not the guiding principle of decisions. An aware person is fully accepting of life as it evolves within and outside oneself and lets the river of life flow unhindered. Research evidence points out that a mindful person is likely to act consistently with his/her intrinsic motivations and values regardless of the external incentives.

People who move at the mercy of their impulses float like a leaf in the currents, letting the currents take them to whatever shore they would reach; they are not the captains of their ships having deliberated and made the mindful decision on their courses or their outcomes. Hence the adage: a life without reflection is not worth living. Integration is not possible without self-awareness and reflection. Mindfulness is an ongoing exercise throughout life. However, the more mindful a person is, the better his or her psycho-spiritual integration.

Mindfulness takes on a distinctive character when we deliberately cultivate an awareness of God's continuous and loving presence in and around us. Faith and appreciation of God's presence is not an intellectual or philosophical notion; it is a deliberately sought experience. It is not a deistic notion of God's omniscience and omnipresence. It is becoming aware that God is the Self of one's self, the ground of one's being. He is the inner light and the source of our life. When we observe ourselves non-judgmentally, we are acquiring the mind of God who watches us with delight, as a mother watches her child. The body is the temple of the Spirit of God, His dwelling place; we become aware of this truth with our mindfulness. The Spirit of God is genuinely present, building His Kingdom deep within us. Self-observation without recognizing God's presence leads to emptiness and a sense of existential futility. It leads us to acknowledge our nothingness and finally to nihilism. Without God in our conscious lives, our existence becomes a meaningless and temporary bubble in the mysterious ocean of life. Self-observation without the contemplation of God's presence in us can lead to severe and persistent existential anxiety, panic attacks, and even suicidal feelings.

Mindfulness is the atmosphere for contemplative prayer. In the quietness of our mind, away from its judgments and evaluations, we seek the presence of God. A mindful prayer centers on God who is seated in the very heart of our being, as its very ground. In such prayer, we do not ask: "Where are you, God?" Instead, we listen to God's constant inquiry: "Where are you," (Adam)? (Gen 3:9). In listening to that question, we observe that we "feel naked" and ashamed. We observe ourselves rationalizing our sinfulness, refusing to be attuned to God's loving destiny and will for us. It is in mindful contemplation we travel with Jesus, Mary, and other characters in the Gospel, and observe our tendencies.

Authenticity

Being true to oneself, being authentic, flows naturally from being mindful. All pretensions aside, there is no defensiveness or attempt to rationalize who we are. A genuine person is transparent to oneself. He or she attempts to act congruently with the sense of self; one is genuinely remorseful at one's failures. There is no denial, minimization, rationalization, etc. of one's shortcomings. They are acknowledged as such. Authenticity calls for a willingness to reform and correct the error of one's ways. On the other hand, it is essential to recognize our successes as such with the profound and humbling awareness that the Lord is indeed behind our success and we praise and glorify Him for what He has accomplished through us.

Socially inappropriate disclosure or transparency of self is not tantamount to being authentic; it can be, in fact, exhibitionism. Authenticity does not deprive persons of their legitimate privacy. A genuine person takes on social roles and wisely withholds aspects of self from others which others have no right to know. As we will see later, authenticity reveals itself in great humility, respect for others, and genuine experiences of inter-dependence and gratitude. An authentic person eschews an inflated or deflated sense of self; there are no pretensions or hypocrisy. Knowledge and awareness of one's authentic self is an asymptotic process. There are aspects of us we do not know. In this regard, the human condition calls for feedback from others. It is in the context of interpersonal relationships and the challenges of life we come to realize aspects of our real self. Others can be a real mirror for us.

Sincerity is not necessarily the same as authenticity; we can deceive ourselves sincerely. A fanatic who cuts the throat of an innocent person may be sincere, but unquestionably not authentic. Authenticity calls for a constant awareness of the possibility that one could be wrong in his or her perceptions and beliefs. Many confuse authenticity with the free expression of emotions and thoughts. "I am telling you the truth; this is how I feel or think," they contend. Dynamic psychology has abundantly demonstrated that our emotional expressions, thought processes, and our reactions can often hide our real motives, which often are unconscious. For example, we may unconsciously hide our true feelings by demonstrating outwardly the very opposite of what we truly feel; this is a mental defense called *reaction formation*. Sometimes people in the name of being true, express them-selves with the unconscious intention of hurting or striking back. Those who cannot handle their hostility towards another could very well develop a *passive aggressive* stance in the name of "peace." These insights of psychol-ogy tell us that mindless expression in the name of "truth" is far from being authentic. The self-righteous Pharisee thought himself to be authentic, but Jesus unambiguously called them hypocrites. The crucial test of authentic expression of self is the manifestation of humility, love and compassion for others, and the courage to be faithful to one's convictions.

We cannot hide from God. This objective sense of transparency to God is a constant spiritual invitation for us to seek our authentic self, the way God sees us, independent of our views of ourselves. Why hide from our-selves, when God sees us exactly as we are? Self-righteousness is the antith-esis of authenticity. It is the ultimate and most destructive self-deception.

A self-righteous person is out of touch with his inner self, while he believes that he knows himself. He insists that God should see him as he considers himself instead of understanding how God sees him. That is why some spiritual writers consider self-righteousness as the most pernicious obstacle to spirituality. "If you were blind, you would not be guilty. But now that you claim to see, you will keep on being guilty." (Jn. 9:41) "The Lord has used his powerful arm to scatter those who are proud." (Lk: 1: 51) The closer we get to God, the greater our authentic sense of self. Left to ourselves we are wretched, wounded, sinful, and unworthy. "Wretched man that I am! Who shall deliver me..?" (Rom.7:24). God saves us from ourselves by His love and sacrifice.

Spontaneity

Authenticity is the ground for spontaneity, a child-like quality that endears us to people. It is at play we are naturally spontaneous. At play, we let ourselves go and experience the sheer pleasure and joy. In this regard, prayer has similar qualities. In true prayer, we can be ourselves and be transparent to God. When we pray we are not continually reminding ourselves that we are praying; instead, we let ourselves go and experience God's presence. Excessive and critical awareness of the fact we are praying during prayer can be a source of desolation and anxiety. Jesus has instructed us to call God, our "Abba" (Father) in heaven. We are asked to approach Him in a child-like manner, which is characterized by spontaneity, playfulness, trust, and innocence. We do not have to be inhibited by anything in our relationship with God. Spiritual masters tell us to enjoy and flow with the experience and only after the fact, reflect on it. As we mature in our relationship with the Lord, we tend to find the most spontaneous way to converse with Him. Cultivating spontaneity with the Lord has a generalizing effect in our daily interactions with others.

A spontaneous person is creative, allows insights to develop, and is uninhibited in self-expression. Such a person refuses to be on "pins and needles" in relationships. The fear of making a mistake does not deter a spontaneous person. Of course, spontaneity is not the same as being foolhardy or impulsive. Spontaneity calls for the uninhibited self-expression in the context of circumspection. Cultural and social inhibitions do not prevent a spontaneous person in exercising appropriately and naturally the legitimate expressions of emotions or creativity. They refuse to be conditioned by other people's expectations. Authenticity and spontaneity go hand in hand. Spontaneous people also are prone to apologize readily when they realize that they have hurt someone.

Intimacy

We are born with the inherent need to experience caring as well as caring for others. Intimacy is the precious experience of a genuine I-Thou relationship where the real self is in contact with the real person of the other. Experience of closeness is enhanced when one cultivates the qualities of awareness, authenticity, and spontaneity. Intimacy creates automatic acceptance of the other as a person and generates the gift of mutual trust. It enhances and confirms love, which in turn deepens intimacy. Intimacy is the foundation for the genuine relationship in the family, friendship, and spirituality.

Genuine intimacy demands that we respect each other's dignity, free agency, and individuality. Closeness does not mean disregard for personal and social boundaries. Intimacy is lost when we try to control and interfere with other people's autonomy and freedom. We express Intimacy in our loving and accepting attitude towards others. We allow others to be themselves with us, authentic and spontaneous, as we present ourselves to them as we are with no pretensions or airs. Intimacy generates love and love creates intimacy.

We experience intimacy in its ultimate form when we relate to God. We are transparent to Him, and God is entirely available to us. However, we can and do create obstacles to this mystical intimacy when we alienate ourselves through deliberate actions that hurt us and others and go against God's revealed will for us. Sin is the state of alienation from intimacy with God. However, even when we are going against God, God continues to be intimate with us through His constant invitation to repent and return to Him. Prayer is the most and readily available forum for us to be intimate with God. When we receive the Lord in the Eucharist, we achieve a greater intimacy where the Lord becomes our very nourishment. Unlike natural food that we assimilate, in the Eucharist, we are absorbed into Him and transformed into members of His mystical body. The Eucharist is the mystery that intimately unites us with the Lord as well as the members of His Church. The ultimate intimacy is our union with the Lord. Closeness to God is the model of genuine interpersonal relationship. Sexual union in the context of permanent commitment and love in marriage is one of the most profound forms of intimacy. It sacramentally represents Christ's union with His Church. Scripture and mystics used the marital union as analogous to the mystical union with God. However, the sexual union can be achieved with pseudo-intimacy almost always leaving the partners in spiritual as well as psychological disarray.

Autonomy

Without the ability for self-determination, the freedom to choose and act on our own behalf, we are no different than the rest of the animal kingdom. The ability to direct one's course, autonomy, is one of our most cherished and jealously guarded attributes. Experience of competence, relatedness, and autonomy are three most important intrinsic motivations of our life. Autonomy is probably the most crucial and foundational among them. Without the experience of self-determination, we cannot achieve a sense of competence or genuine relatedness. Autonomy is intimately connected with intelligence, especially the ability to distinguish right from wrong. In one sense, autonomy has no meaning if we lack rationality and understanding. It is precisely because we are endowed with intelligence, we should have the ability to act accordingly. We cannot hold a person responsible for his or her actions, if they were mentally incapable of understanding the nature and seriousness of their actions or could not distinguish right from wrong. In many ways we choose who we are and how we act. In that sense we create ourselves because of our intelligence and autonomy. When emotions control our actions against reason, we lose autonomy. Excessive dependence on others is another condition that destroys autonomy. Autonomy obviously does not mean we act whimsically or simply as we feel. Practice of virtue and the vigorous exercise of our values are known to enhance our sense of freedom and autonomy. In fact, there is no freedom without virtue. When we are externally regulated by events, people, and laws that are inherently unjust, etc. we feel oppressed and violated. However, when we internalize external demands as consistent with our internal value systems and regulate our activities accordingly, we only enhance our sense of autonomy. The commandments of God, the prescriptions of the Church, just laws in civil society, and the commonly accepted codes of behavior—all these are necessary to preserve our autonomy. They are like good brakes on an automobile. Without the brakes the car cannot be driven safely. The sounder the brake-system, the freer we feel in driving the car in the direction we want it to go.

Self-efficacy as an important concept related to autonomy and self-determination. Self-efficacy is the belief that one can achieve a result through one's actions. It has been shown by research, primarily by Dr. Albert Bandura, that a strong sense of self-efficacy produces more magnificent achievement and self-satisfaction. Therefore, it is easy to see that self-efficacy influences our motivation, emotions, and thoughts. Since self-efficacy is an essential concept, we will elaborate some of the core issues related to its function. Self-efficacy involves a willingness to be aware of and reflect on one's core beliefs about self; second, it requires an ability to regulate one's emotions and activities in the light of the goal one is trying to achieve; thirdly, it demands patience and persistence in the effort. Human autonomy reaches its fulfillment through self-efficacy. If one does not believe that he or she cannot achieve a goal, it is useless to talk about independence in that regard. Freedom is not only an exercise in choice but also the vehicle to reach a chosen goal. As can be seen, self-efficacy and psycho-spiritual integration are interrelated. A well-integrated person demonstrates the qualities required to have self-efficacy.

Discussion of self-efficacy might appear to some as contradicting the fundamental attitude of "spiritual poverty" or total dependence on God. If self-efficacy is essentially a belief in one's own ability to achieve the desired goal, how can such a person depend on God? Upon reflection, it is not difficult to see that this is a pseudo-dilemma. Dependence on God does not contradict our belief that God has endowed us with abilities and talents. In fact, grateful recognition of God and His continuing empowerment of our beings give us the self-confidence that otherwise we would not have. "The builders build in vain unless the Lord builds with them." A soldier who fights the battle is not lessened in his morale or confidence by recalling that he has a powerful general guiding the war. Self-determination and autonomy independent of the recognition of the Lord as our master is a pursuit that results in ultimate futility. Psycho-spiritual integration of a Christian is in the Poverty of Spirit which brings the "inheritance of the Kingdom of God." For a Christian, self-efficacy is the faith that God accomplishes great things through his or her inherently weak undertakings. "Through Him, I can accomplish all things." "For he who is mighty has done great things for me, holy is his name."(Lk:1:49) "Therefore, my beloved brothers, be steadfast, immovable, always abounding in the work of the Lord, knowing that in the Lord your labor is not in vain."(1Cor:1:58) Self-efficacy, in fact, increases as we know that the all-powerful and loving God wants us to succeed in the endeavors that are worthy of Him and us. He is the primary source of our inner strength. He is the Lord Charioteer, while Arjuna fights the battle.

Autonomy, as well as self-efficacy, is not pure self-agency in practice. We are social and interrelated beings. We accomplish many things through and by the willing help of others. Part of self-efficacy is the belief that one can achieve specific goals only in collaboration with others and society at large. We also render others self-efficacious through our partnership and support. We make ourselves as our community also creates us. A sense of autonomy or self-confidence independent of our interdependence can lead us to an anti-social stance, the extreme of which manifests in the structure of anti-social personality disorder. The sociopath does not believe that he can ever depend on others, much less God, in anything concerning his welfare; he thinks that he must fend for himself often exploiting and brutalizing his victims. He may have a false sense of self-efficacy; however, ultimately he renders himself a defective and sick individual.

Openness

Openness is the quality of the mind that is willing and eager to learn, knowing that we do not know everything. It opens the door to the deepening of what we know and the exploration of what is yet to be understood. It clears the pathway for reforming the error of our ways through feedback from those who observe us. Openness helps us to be genuinely remorseful when we discover that we were wrong; it makes it easy for us to forgive ourselves as well as others. A person with a closed mind and heart is as good as fossilized. Openness and receptivity flourish in a person who is self-aware, humble, intimate, and free.

The receptivity that goes with the quality of openness is the foundational attitude for receiving the gift of faith. The seeds of faith, the Word of God, cannot grow on the rocky grounds of close-mindedness. The incident of the cure of the blind man in John's Gospel (Jn.9) illustrates this. The cured blind man tells the Pharisees: "If this man were not from God, he could do nothing." (Jn.9:33) The Pharisees answered: "You were born in utter sin, and would you teach us?" Jesus declared to them when they asked, "Are we also blind?" Jesus said to them, "If you were blind, you would have no guilt; but now that you say, 'We see,' your guilt remains." (Jn. 9:46-48). Self-righteousness destroys openness and renders us blind. Transparency is the very condition on which psycho-spiritual integration depends.

Naiveté and gullibility are not the same as openness. They are signs of immaturity and lack of personal convictions. An unwillingness to actively search for the truth and laziness to succumb to the immediate persuasions are factors that foster naiveté and gullibility. Such people are reeds shaking in the wind as it blows in every direction. They take no personal responsibility for establishing solid foundations for their inner convictions. They fall easy victims to every theory or fashion that come along. St. Paul rebukes the Galatians for their quick acceptance of false preaching: "I am astonished that you are so quickly deserting him who called you in the grace of Christ and are turning to a different gospel...But even if an angel from heaven or we should preach to you a gospel contrary to the one we preached to you, let him be accursed." (Gal: 1:6-9). Openness calls for dialogue and a willingness to change one's position in the light of new evidence.

While gullibility is an absence of personal convictions, even a convinced person can be deceived and ultimately persuaded into taking a wrong position, an instance of "sincere" deception. "And no wonder, for even Satan disguises himself as an angel of light..." (2Cor. 11:14). Openness calls for vigilance and discrimination. One needs to examine the origin, process, and end of a new persuasion. Discernment of Spirits calls for an honest examination of the end-result of a new position. "Their end will correspond to their deeds."(2Cor. 11:15) A well-integrated person is open and honest, but not easily persuaded.

CHAPTER 7

Discernment of the Spirits

Beloved, do not believe every spirit but test the spirits to see whether they are from God, for many false prophets have gone into the world. By this, you know the Spirit of God: every spirit that confesses that Jesus Christ has come in the flesh is from God, and every spirit that does not confess Jesus is not from God. (1Jn 4: 2, 3)

Among the mature, we do impart wisdom, although it is not a wisdom of this age or of the rulers of this age, who are doomed to pass away. But we impart a secret and hidden wisdom of God, which God decreed before the ages for our glory. (1Cor 2: 6, 7)

The Spiritual Exercises of St. Ignatius of Loyola is a masterpiece in mystical literature. The Spiritual Exercises has been the mainstay of Jesuit spirituality and the fountain from which sprang the holy lives of numerous saints and martyrs. In the Spiritual Exercises, St. Ignatius gives fourteen plus eight "rules" of spiritual discernment, an invaluable treasure of practical guidance in discerning the spiritual movements, especially in one's prayer life. St. Ignatius speaks in the language of his period. Modern psychology has enriched our understanding of the dynamics of the human psyche; however, it is remarkable how penetrating the insights of St. Ignatius were. The following discussion of the discernment of Spirits, an essential process in the psycho-spiritual integrative endeavor, is primarily inspired and guided by the insights provided in the Spiritual Exercises.

We can broadly divide the spirits at work in our lives into four: the Spirit of God and His holy angels, the evil spirits, the spirit of the world, and the human spirit. It must be made clear that the word "spirit" is applied here broadly. The good spirits are the Holy Spirit and His holy angels. The evil spirits are the Devil and his fallen companions. These are beings with intelligence and freedom, even though the evil spirits have irrevocably employed their freedom to defy God and to fight against His loving plan for us. The spirit of the world is neither an individual nor a principle of being but nebulously defined as a "culture," an attitude, a philosophy, etc. having an existence and profound influence in the history and culture of humankind. Saint Ignatius categorizes the spiritual forces at work in our psyche into Good and Evil Spirits. The saint seems to have implied that the evil spirits employ the worldly spirit as a tool. The battle is about the human spirit who is the object of influence here; however, the human spirit is not a passive object, but a subject with its free agency and therefore can, and does, collaborate, and choose to resist or succumb to the influences of the other spirits. The human person is ultimately accountable for the way he or she chooses to interact with the other spiritual influences in life.

The Spirit of God and His good Angels

The Holy Spirit is God, the third person of the Triune God. He is the Paraclete, the Advocate, the Counselor, and the Helper the Lord had promised to send upon His ascension (Jn. 14:16). The ascension signified the official end of the Lord's bodily ministry; henceforth we shall experience His continuing presence and worship Him in "Spirit and Truth." We have entered a formal period of history in which the Holy Spirit is the mover and the pervasive light, guide, and source of life and its continual renewal. He guides the Church infallibly in living and witnessing to the Gospel of the Lord. The Spirit indeed inaugurated "His era" in history in a most remarkable way on the day of Pentecost, inviting all humankind to listen to the proclamation of the Gospel. The Holy Spirit is the vital source of the Church, the Mystical Body and the Bride of Christ.

> *And I will ask the Father, and he will give you another Counselor, to be with you forever, even the Spirit of truth, whom the world cannot receive because it neither sees him nor knows him, you know him, for he dwells with you, and will be in you. (Jn. 14:16-17)*

The Holy Spirit transforms the face of the earth with His seven-fold gifts. He is the giver of life and our spiritual consolation. He is always present as the enlightener, the light that shines in the darkness, the divine inner guide who helps us to know Jesus deeply, to love Him more intimately, and to follow Him more closely. Mother Angelica states: "The Holy Spirit sees our thoughts, hears our sighs, and fulfills our desires. The very Breath of God breathes within us, for we are His living temple."

> *If the Spirit of him who raised Jesus from the dead dwells in you, he who raised Christ Jesus from the dead will also give life to your mortal bodies through his Spirit who dwells in you. It is the Spirit himself bearing witness with our spirit that we are children of God…Likewise, the Spirit helps us in our weakness: for we do not know how to pray for as we ought, but the Spirit himself intercedes for us with sighs too deep for words. And he who searches hearts of men knows what is the mind of the Spirit because the Spirit intercedes for the saints according to the will of God. (Rom 8: 11- 27)*

It is scripturally sound and in keeping with the sacred tradition of the Church to know and believe in the agency of holy angels. Scripture unambiguously tells us that angels intervene in our lives as messengers of God. Our Blessed Mother is the prime example; she gave her momentous *fiat* to God through the agency of angel Gabriel. Angels were present at the Annunciation of John the Baptist's conception; an angel guided St. Joseph, both before and after the birth of Our Lord; angels sang together at the birth of Christ; angels guided the Magi away from the murderous Herod; angels ministered to the Lord after His temptation; they were His comfort at the time of His agony; they stood guard at His tomb upon His triumphant resurrection; they addressed the dazed apostles gazing on to the skies at the ascension…etc. We have no reason to assume that they have ceased to be active in our lives, especially in our spiritual battles deep within our psyche. One thing is sure, inspiration or guidance from a holy angel is always consistent with God's will and the Word of God. How do you discern whether a prompting is from a holy angel or the evil one? St. Paul tells us in Galatians (1:8) that even a seemingly angelic message contrary to the revealed truth of the Gospel should be rejected as wrong.

The message is clear; anything that is contrary to the Word of God or the authentic teachings of the Church cannot be from a good angel.

The Evil Spirits

Your adversary, the devil, prowls around like a roaring lion, seeking someone to devour. Resist him, firm in your faith, knowing that your brotherhood is experiencing the same kinds of suffering throughout the world. And after you have suffered a little while, the God of all grace, who has called you to his eternal glory in Christ, will himself restore, confirm, strengthen, and establish you. (1Pet 5:8-10)

The Spirit of Evil is real and is personified in the fallen angel, the Devil. The devil is a personal being, called by the Lord as the "evil one"; we are taught by the Lord to pray to the Father that we are delivered from "the evil one." (*Gaudete et exsultate* # 160 and 161) He is known by different names, Beelzebub, Satan, the Father of Lies, etc. Even the Lord was not spared from the Devil's onslaught. At the crucial time of the Lord's entry into His public life, the Devil was present, tempting Jesus, persuading Him from His God-appointed path. The Devil is incredibly intelligent and clever, often quoting the very Word of God; he can adapt to circumstances like a chameleon. The Devil is not alone in his evil operations. A host of angels fell with him in their defiance of God. These demonic spirits work with the Devil. Additionally, as we see later, the Devil has successfully manipulated the "world" in creating a cultural atmosphere that is antithetical to God, His Gospel, and His Church.

The Spirit of the "World"

The term "world" is used with varied meanings in the Scripture depending on the context, at times very positive (Jn.3:16), and at other, very negative. For our purposes we understand the word "world" in its circumscribed meaning regarding the "spirit of the world" that is distinct from and opposed to the wisdom and message of the Gospel, as illustrated by the passages below:

...even the Spirit of truth, whom the world cannot receive, because it neither sees him nor knows him (Jn.14:16, 17)

If the world hates you, know that it had hated me before it hated you. If you were of the world, the world would love you as its own; but because you are not of the world, but I chose you out of the world; therefore the world hates you (Jn. 15:18, 19).

And you were dead in the trespasses and sins in which you once walked, following the course of this world, following the prince of the power of the air, the spirit that now at work in the sons of disobedience—among whom we all once lived in the passions of flesh...(Eph. 2: 2-4)

Now we have received not the spirit of the world, but the Spirit who is from God. And we impart this in words not taught by human wisdom but taught by the Spirit, interpreting spiritual truths to those who are spiritual. (1Cor. 2:12, 13)

Do not love the world or the things in the world. If anyone loves the world, the love of the Father is not in him. For all that is in the world—the desires of the flesh and the desires of the eyes and pride in possessions—is not from the Father but is from the world. And the world is passing away along with its attractions, but whoever does the will of God abides forever. (1Jn. 2: 15-17)

Do not be conformed to this world but be transformed by the renewal of your mind, that you may prove what the will of God is, what is good and acceptable and perfect (Rom.12:2)

We know that we are from God, and the whole world lies in the power of the evil one. (1Jn. 5:19)

"But take heart; I have overcome the world." (Jn. 16:33)

"The spirit of the world" is the endemic cultural condition that alienates humanity from God. It relies on the "wisdom of the world" which God made "foolish" (ICor. 1:20) It is a human-centered culture, a spirit, in which "man is the measure of all things." It is the opposite of God's choices

(1Cor 1: 27). The worldly spirit arose out of man's disobedience, resistance to conform to the will of God, the intention to build his own "tower of Babel," etc., creating a perpetuating, habituated, cultural attitude throughout human history antithetical to God's economy of salvation. The worldly spirit is pervasive and penetrates every aspect of human culture, at times in obvious ways, at other in the most subtle manner. The "worldly spirit" is the cockles that the "enemy" has sawed among the wheat; they are almost indistinguishable from the wheat. The Lord allows them to grow, lest the wheat be destroyed along with them if they are pulled out prematurely (Mt 13:24-30). When it is not subtle and indistinguishable, it manifests loudly as the "will to power," considering Christianity as the excuse for cowardice and obsequiousness (Nietzsche).

In reality, the "world" does not acknowledge God, much less accept His Word, "because it neither sees him nor knows him" (Jn. 14: 16, 17). The fundamental evil is to refuse to acknowledge the truth of God, much less the need for God. At its best, it masquerades a humanistic love and advocates worldly prosperity and peace. At its worst, it manifests utter selfishness, avarice, envy, lust for pleasure and power, naked aggression, exploitation, and war. "For all that is in the world—the desires of the flesh and the desires of the eyes and pride in possessions—is not from the Father but is from the world." (1Jn2: 15-17). In one sense it is a subtle and godless religion, a philosophy that believes that "what works is true." It even has "spirituality" devoid of Spirit, "human wisdom" that neither satisfies the mind nor the soul. It is an attitude that claims as its goal the "happiness" of man, but in truth perpetuates misery and marginalizes the poor and needy. It promises freedom and peace, without being able to deliver them. It is at heart, at once atheistic, agnostic and skeptical. It does not acknowledge that "the whole world lies in the power of the evil one" (1Jn. 5:19) because it does not believe in the existence of the Devil, for that matter, anything supernatural.

We will naturally not exhaust the elaboration of the nature and dynamics of the "world." Suffice it to say, that we are born into this "world" and are profoundly influenced by its dynamics, "among all these we all once

lived…and so we by nature children of wrath, like the rest of humankind."
(Eph. 2:3) The Word of God warns us against this "darkness" and ask us to
be "wise as serpents" in dealing with it while maintaining our innocence.
Jesus and His apostles have predicted that the "world" will persecute the
followers of Christ. "Do not be overcome by evil, but overcome evil with
good" (Rom. 12:21). However, the Lord assured us: "Blessed are those who
are persecuted for righteousness sake, for theirs is the kingdom of heaven"
(Mt. 5:10). The Lord also assures us that He has overcome the "world," and
we must "take heart" in that fact. (Jn. 16:33)

The Human Spirit

A human person is an intimate unity of spirit and body. The body,
while alive, is the visibility of our soul which is spiritual. The human spirit
is created to be free with intelligence and inherent moral sense. A human
being is a free agent with the capacity for self-determination. Precisely
because of this freedom, evil is also at hand. Despite its inherent orien-
tation to God and the good, the human spirit can choose the contrary,
to its everlasting destruction. To complicate the matter, we experience an
inherited vitiation, an "original" tendency to be weak in our moral choices.

> For I do not understand my actions. For I do not do what I want,
> but I do the very thing I hate…For I do not do the good I want, but
> the evil I do not want is what I keep on doing…Wretched man that
> I am! Who will deliver me from this body of death? (Rom 7: 13-24)

This experiential fact illustrates an aspect of the dogma of "original sin.
The Catechism of the Catholic Church states:

> The doctrine of original sin is the "reverse side" of the Good News
> that Jesus is the Savior of all men that all need salvation and that
> salvation is offered to all through Christ. The Church, which has
> the mind of Christ, knows very well that we cannot tamper with
> the revelation of original sin without undermining the mystery of
> Christ. (422)

Modern depth psychology has tried to explore the original human condition concerning the structure of the human psyche. The analysts tell us that the human psyche is born with an unhindered cauldron of impulses and drives. As the impulses emerge as desires, drives, urges, and fantasies, the individual is confronted with realities of life, both within, and outside, that curb their unhindered expression. As we mature in our capacity to evaluate reality critically, our impulse-driven aspect of the psyche is forced to conform to external and internalized demands, thus creating standards of verbal and behavioral expressions, indeed culture and morality. Such pressures build in us the faculties or structures such as "ego" and "super-ego." While the behavioral expressions are "normalized" to the standards and values of the society, regardless whether such were internalized or not, the power of the impulses does not necessarily diminish. They are "always" there, waiting for an opportunity or "excuse" to come out. The expressions of these instinctive impulses produce an experience of release, which we experience as pleasure. Such pleasures are self-reinforcing, prompting repetition. We employ an array of mental defenses to ward off the intrusion of these "unacceptable" and "undesirable" impulses into our awareness. The inherent conflicts these impulses create *vis-a-vis* the demands of our conscience, society, and our deliberate goals, etc. are sources of anxiety. The human spirit experiences them as a "wretched state" of perpetual bondage. St. Paul is no exception to this experience as he vividly confesses to the conflict in spiritual terms.

However, the human mind is very tricky indeed! It has the proven capacity to yield to its underlying and powerful impulses in deceptive ways. It can naively or with sophisticated arguments deny the obvious; it can rationalize, or amazingly convert one impulse to appear as its opposite, etc. Relaxed self-awareness and careful examination of the movement of one's spirit are essential to get to the truth of our lives. An interesting, and often tragic, turn of events is that we blame the Devil for our misbehavior or undue inner promptings. The-Devil-made-me-do-it defense is known to humankind from the inception as illustrated in the behavior of our first parents even as they were losing paradise. They blamed each other and the Devil. There was no discernment that their spirits deceived them more than the Devil. They did not feel sorry, because they did not take responsibility for their misdeeds; instead, they experienced "shame," an ontological, primitive, and unproductive feeling of unworthiness. They forgot that they were the loving and glorious creations of God who made them in His very image. Sure, they were aggrieved; but it was not grief that moved them to repentance and life, but a "worldly guilt" that brought forth death. "For godly grief produces a repentance that leads to salvation without regret, whereas worldly grief produces death." (2Cor 7:10)

Another consideration in this matter is the human spirit's inherent self-centeredness, which psychologists categorize as narcissism. The truth of our lives tells us that love prompts our redemption and fulfillment; however, we tend to hold on to ourselves to the marginalization and sometimes the total exclusion of others. The natural tendency to grow and develop our full potential is not selfishness but our God-given duty. On the other hand, a person, because of a debilitating sense of lack of self-affirmation, or because of overindulgence that deprived him of the opportunity to experience individuation can become pathologically self-preoccupied. This type of narcissism reveals a partially formed self, unconsciously experiencing a profound sense of profound emptiness, which is defended by grandiosity, lack of empathy, entitlement, self-idealization, etc. Deliberately cultivated selfishness to the exclusion of others, an unwillingness to let go of self with courage and love, leads ultimately to the very destruction of the person.

> *"If anyone would come after me, let him deny himself and take up his cross and follow me. For whoever would save his life will lose it, but whoever loses his life will find it. For what will it profit a man if he gains the whole world and forfeits his soul? Or what shall a man give in return for his soul?" (Mt 16: 24-26).*

Selfishness arises from a lack of appreciation of our communal nature and interdependence. Selfishness militates against the fact that we are created in the image of a Thrice-personal God who is one substance in three relationships of total love. When we are faithful to our beings, we demonstrate the Trinitarian life in action.

The spiritual States and Related Movements

The spirits move depending on the state of the human soul and the disposition of the psyche. In spiritual terms, we may broadly distinguish the status of the human soul in three basic categories: the evil, tepid, and militant states. The spirits are at work in all the three in very different ways.

The "evil" or corrupt state

The corrupt state is when a person has deliberately chosen to go from good to bad, or bad to worse. This sinful state alienates the person from God and fellow human beings. The corrupt state is on a course of deterioration and spiritual death. Such a person has dulled the voice of his conscience and is increasingly in danger of a fatal choice of total rejection of God, or worse, a blasphemous severing of one's openness to the Grace of the Holy Spirit. This defiant and deliberate reversal of truth, an unforgivable state of mind, as stated in the Scriptures, is the most dangerous. (Mt. 12:3; Mk. 3:28; Lk. 12:10; Is. 5:20).

The Devil is the cheerleader here. He works with the human spirit to conjure up images of great pleasure, sensuality, wealth, power, etc. consistent with the uncensored tendencies of the person. He provides every type of rationalization, excuses, obfuscations and denials, consistent with the "worldly spirit", in order to silence the conscience. The person is falling into the bottomless pit of desire and lust…The comfort the evil Spirit provides to the person obviously is jarringly short-lived and ultimately unfulfilling. As Saint Ignatius describes it, it is like a drop of water falling on a rock. The evil spirits work with the human spirit prompting it to yield to its impulses, asking it to turn a deaf ear to the groaning of its conscience, declaring the death of God, the nullity of the belief in life after death, and eventually destroying faith in the risen Lord and the credibility of His Church. Such a person is an easy prey and a direct hit for the Devil. He or she is akin to the crucified criminal on the left of the Lord, asking: "Are you not the Christ? Save yourself and us!" (Lk. 23:39). The evil Spirit may even encourage the unfortunate soul to blame the Devil for its misdeeds, encouraging the soul to find comfort in the displacement of responsibility, thereby deceiving the person even deeper! As the person accelerates in evil ways, the Devil may introduce a sense of irreversibility, unworthiness, and despair. The person is brought to feel eventually that he cannot be redeemed even if he wants to. That is the Devil's ultimate victory over the soul: take away any hope of redemption. Such a person is under the influence of the "world" and lives a life consistent with worldly values, antithetical to God's plan for him or her. Such a person is subject to psychological conflict and distress. He or she does not experience inner peace; life may appear meaningless and futile.

In this situation, the good spirits work in the opposite direction. Through the biting of conscience, the good spirits will agitate the mind, and try to create anxiety and ego-dystonia. Self-induced suffering may be used to confront the individual as to the consequences of his or her own choices in life. Spirit, like a loving parent, chides the wayward son or daughter, trying to turn the person around (convert). He agitates the spirit, takes away the comfort and joy (desolation). On such occasions human beings tend to hide from God ask the silly question: "Where is God?" instead of asking, "Where am I?" (Gen 3:9). We need to discern the voice of God and listen to His pained query: "Where are you?" Naturally, one can infer the tactics of the evil Spirit on those occasions, prompting one to doubt the existence of God and indulge oneself fulfilling one's wayward fantasies.

The Tepid State

The Tepid State is one of disengagement and disinterest in spiritual life. The person has taken a lackadaisical approach of "Que Sera, Sera" and refuses to take an active interest in cultivating his spiritual life. He is the servant who buried his talent (Mt. 24:24).

> *"Master, I knew you to be a hard man, reaping where you did not sow, and gathering where you did not winnow, so I was afraid, and I went and hid your talent in the ground. Here, you have what is yours."*

It may appear as laziness, but it is indeed a fear of failure and account-ability. It is passive resistance to acknowledging the gifts of life and an active refusal to cultivate them. There is no celebration, much less a willingness to accept the challenge. Such a person is a "taker" and not a "giver." This passive-aggressive approach creates natural resentment in those who look up to that person, seeing that he or she is unwilling to come through with their responsibility. Such persons rationalize their manner of existence by falsely comforting themselves that they are not doing anything seriously wrong. They are neither "fish nor fowl."

> *"I know your works: you are neither cold nor hot. Would that you were cold or hot! So, because you are lukewarm and neither cold nor hot, I will spew you out of my mouth. For you say, I am rich, I have prospered, and I need nothing; not knowing that you are wretched, pitiable, miserable, blind, and naked. (Rev. 3:15-17)*

It is a state of soul that does not experience any spiritual passion and is satisfied with the minimum. They may attend church resentfully; they sacrifice little and do not show generosity. They are secretly self-indulgent and lives a life of venial violations, taking comfort that they do not commit "big" sins. Their spiritual state may be compared to a low-grade fever, undetectable and causing no panic or immediate attention. But as it is said "a soul does not lie where it falls"; it is insidious erosion and a gradual falling into the ravine. In spiritual life not progressing is the same as going backward.

> *The point is this: he who sows sparingly will also reap sparingly, and he who sows bountifully will also reap bountifully. Each one must do as he has made up his mind, not reluctantly or under compulsion, for God loves a cheerful giver. (2Cor. 9:6, 7)*

The tepid soul loves sparingly and is not a cheerful giver. He or she is resentful and feels imposed upon. They would bury their responsibility than accept and fulfill it.

The passivity of the tepid soul is potentially dangerous. They start small fires that can ultimately cause devastation. "How great a forest is set ablaze by a small fire!" (James 3:5). The venial existence of the tepid soul manifested by a life of "petty sins," distractions, passive aggression, minimal involvement, etc., may cause significant harm without their directly intending it.

As is apparent the evil spirit knows that it cannot persuade the tepid soul into obvious iniquity. So it quietly leaves the soul in this "low-grade fever" of gradual degradation waiting for a chance to pounce and to devour him or her. He "patiently" roams around the weakly built fortress looking for the weakest spot to strike.

The worldly spirit has permeated the tepid soul insidiously. The tepid soul lives a subtle mundane life without overtly or consciously committing to its atheistic values. He or she "takes enough insurance" to be not outright displeasing to God, in case He exists!

The good spirits are active in agitating the tepid soul; through desolations and aridity, they confront the lackadaisical soul, encouraging it to wake up.

> *Therefore I counsel you to buy from me gold refined in fire… Those whom I love, I reprove and chasten; so be zealous and repent. Behold, I stand at the door and knock; if anyone hears my voice and opens the door, I will come to him and eat with him, and he with me. (Rev.3:18-22)*

The Militant State

Spiritual life is a life of militancy, a constant battle. The natural impulses bombard the human psyche; the "world" permeates every aspect of its life; the evil spirits are on the prowl waiting for every opportunity to tempt and vitiate; the good spirits are vigilant with their holy inspirations. Fortunately, where sin has abounded, Grace has abounded even more. When we exclaim "wretched man that I am! Who will deliver me from this body of death?" the answer is immediate and ready: "Thanks be to God, through Jesus Christ our Lord!" (Rom.7:24, 25). The militant state of a holy soul is awake, mindful, and attentive. Spiritual vigilance is our duty because while we are justified in Christ and are assured of the way to salvation, we must work out (bring to completion) our salvation in reverence and total obedience to God (Phil. 2:12). While we are still sojourning on this earth, we have the ability and freedom to deviate from the path shown by God; temptations are many. Sure, the Lord has saved us by his pure and unmerited love; but we retain the capacity to reject Him, even after we have once accepted it. Human life is spread out in time and space; until the very end, we cannot gather it into one moment. We can lose it between the cup and the lip. We cannot be complacent; we must "press on" and be faithful.

> I am astonished that you are so quickly deserting him who called you in the grace of Christ and turning to a different gospel—not that there is another gospel (Gal. 1:6)

We can go wrong, even after accepting the salvation assured by the Lord; we can apostatize, become recalcitrant.

> Therefore let anyone who thinks that he stands, take heed lest he falls. No temptation has overtaken you that is not common to man. God is faithful, and he will not let you be tempted beyond your strength, but with the temptation will also provide the way of escape, that you may be able to endure it (1Cor. 10:12, 13)

We are warned to be vigilant and watchful. "Watch and pray that you may not enter into temptation; the spirit indeed is willing, but the flesh is weak" (Mk. 14:38). Again, "Fight the good fight of faith; take hold of the eternal life to which you were called when you made the good confession in the presence of many witnesses" (1Tim. 6:12). The numerous and constant warnings in the Scriptures remind us of the dangers and the need for perseverance in the faith.

The tactics of the spirits with those who are spiritually moving from good to better vary depending on the situation. The good spirits are the cheerleaders here. God visits these souls with his constant grace, efficaciously filling them with the manifold gifts of the Holy Spirit, spiritual consolation, inner peace, and fortitude. "God is light, and in him is no darkness at all." (1Jn. 1:5) For those who are tending towards good, the Spirit makes His presence felt sweetly and gently, unambiguously with joy and consolation. As the master of discernment, St. Ignatius of Loyola, poetically puts it, He comes as "water on a sponge". He is in the quiet after the "wind" and the "thunder". He is in the "burning bush" of our souls, without destroying it. The presence of the Lord is unmistakable, while the imposters are harder to discern. When we are moved in our hearts to believe and surrender to God, to tears contemplating the unfathomable love of the Father, to proclaim and praise the name of the Lord, it is the Spirit of God. For no one can proclaim Jesus is Lord without the Spirit. The fruits He bears in us are sweet and fragrant, wisdom, understanding, counsel, fortitude, knowledge, piety and fear of the Lord (Is. 11:2-3). On a rarer note, He could blindingly reveal His light to us, as Paul of Tarsus experienced. When God visits "without cause" there is no doubt attached to it. Inner peace and harmony in relationships, a peace that the world cannot give, is the gift of the Spirit. We know when we have it. When the Spirit of God moves us we deepen our faith and commitment, our hopes are renewed and confirmed, and our love is made more intimate and productive.

The evil spirit is the direct adversary here. He might try a frontal attack; he would plant doubts in the mind of the militant soul, suggesting with the aid of the worldly spirit that it is impossible to persevere in such a course and that one cannot keep up the vigilant pace. He tries to plant resentment of the "rules," suggesting that they are too hard and demanding. The evil spirit makes the soul compare his or her struggles with those who have it "easy"; tempts the soul by showing how others are "enjoying" a celebratory life in the world, etc. If the bad spirit fails to succeed outright, he approaches the soul subtly by trying to slow down his or her progress in spiritual life, bring them to a life of tepidity. He minimizes the gravity of venial failures and keeps the person down from the flight upwards. He may introduce a sense of "achievement" and self-righteousness, the deadly sin of pride.

While in the above situations there are no ambiguities, we are in the midst of a deceptive atmosphere when the evil presents itself as an "angel of light," or a false prophet appears in our lives in "sheep's clothing but inwardly are ravenous wolves" (Mt 7: 15-19). They pretend to be from God and attempts to take on deceitful airs and signs. On such occasions, we are asked to turn "stones into bread," "jump from the pinnacle," or "try to be the emperor of the world"--all in the name of God Himself! Human history has abundantly shown many such instances of miraculous visions, fabulous interpretations of the Scripture, "sincere" criticisms of the Church, and such. The fanatic who cuts the throat of the innocent, the "holy warrior" who terrorizes in the name of the Holy One, the crusader who burned children alive, the inquisitionist who burned Joan of Arc…are clear instances of "holy" deception.

If a frontal attack or overt deception does not work, the evil spirit will try to enter through the 'front door' of the militant soul, appearing to be an advocate for 'holiness.' He will "inspire" the soul with accelerated spiritual practices, such as increasing spiritual practices, undue fasting regimen, exhibitionism of religiosity, neurotic guilt, etc. He will try to convince the soul that they have truly "arrived" and on the way to living sainthood. He may try to make soul uncharitably zealous in viewing others critically for "not measuring up." Worse still, the evil spirit may visit those souls with false visions, exhibitionistic and miraculous and prophetic powers, theological "insights," criticism of superiors or the failures of Church, etc. The Lord has instructed us to look to the fruits on such occasions, instead of looking at the seemingly green leaves of the tree. "You will recognize them by their fruits" (Mt 7:19). "Either make the tree good and its fruit good, or make the tree bad and its fruit bad, for the tree is known by its fruit" (Mt 12: 33)

Self-righteousness, as we have already discussed earlier, is a source of great deception. The self-righteous might glory in their prayer-life, sacrifices, and faithfulness to the Law, believing that the Spirit of God is on their side. Regarding spiritual discernment, this is the most subtle and difficult to discriminate and overcome. The self-righteous resentfully stands "outside," unable to participate in the celebrations of joy, complaining about the feast given to the prodigal. "If we say we have no sin, we deceive ourselves, and the truth is not in us." (1Jn. 1:8) As St. Ignatius of Loyola reminds us, the closer we get to God, the higher our awareness of our sins. The self-righteous person moves in the opposite direction. The evil spirit is content with a self-righteous person. He is likely to leave him or her alone in their dangerous self-sufficiency and complacency.

The evil spirit fills his arsenal with sharp and sometimes extremely subtle weapons, that can deceive even the spiritually experienced persons. In this regard, God may allow, for a different purpose, trials, and tribulations to purify the soul in "fire" and catapult the person into a deeper love and imitation of the Lord. Saints have described "spiritual nights,"experiences of the absence of the Lord. Fortunately, such difficult trials are permitted only at the level of the spiritual strength of the soul; God never visits us with tribulations beyond what we can bear. "And after you have suffered a little while, the God of all grace, who has called you to his eternal glory in Christ, will himself restore, confirm, strengthen, and establish you." (1Pet. 5:8-10)

We experience desolation when we no longer experience the sweetness of God's presence. It is as if we are left to fend for ourselves. St. Ignatius instructs us on those occasions to scrutinize ourselves. The Ninth Rule of the Spiritual Exercises states that there are three possible reasons for the experience of desolation. 1. we have become lackadaisical or negligent in our spiritual life; 2. to help us to see the strength of our commitment and willingness to serve without the felt joy; 3. to remind us that we are not the source of our power, much less of the spiritual joy; God is. During periods of desolation, we are instructed not to make or change significant decisions about our lives, except to increase our commitment to pursue our spiritual journey zealously.

Even the Lord went through unspeakable agony before His passion in Gethsemane as his human soul confronted the impending and ignominious suffering and death. All the spirits might have been active in that awesome moment pushing and pulling the God-man in every direction, making Him sweat blood. As He was hanging on the cross, the Lord cried with the Psalmist: "My God, my God, why have you forsaken me?"(Ps. 22:1; Mk. 15:34).

In this context it may be useful to reflect on the mystery-affirmation in the Apostles Creed: "He descended into hell." Jesus did not spare himself from any human experience, with the exception of committing sin. Of all human experience, perhaps, the most painful and frightening is death and the fear of ending up as nothing or worse, in hell. In popular conceptions hell is described in anthropomorphic terms as a place of torture through "fire and brimstone". Hell is the state of being, consequent of an assertion and practice of total self-sufficiency, rejecting the ontological dependence on the Creator and Father. This is the loneliest and isolated stance a human being can decide to adopt, contrary to his very nature as a related being, a being *for* others, above all, *for* God. We are created in the image of the Thrice-personal God in total love. Our destiny and salvation is in this relationship. Hell is the total absence and unmitigated contradiction to what a human being is destined to be. Death may be seen as the loneliest and most "stinging" experience of the definitive destruction of all relatedness, a descent into a state of "non-being". We are told that Jesus experienced this, as a human being, by dying, "descending into hell". God died as man. He truly descended into hell to conquer it, proving that love conquers death and is stronger than death. He rose as the glorious Lord and the "first fruit" thereby definitively destroying the power of death in our lives. In spiritual life, we may be allowed to "descend" into hell, precisely to be able to experience and exercise the power of love and relationship with God and fellow human beings. Desolation of this type is possible for the very holy souls, as demonstrated and narrated to us by holy mystics and saints. While total self-reliance is hell, total acceptance and dependence on God's gift of Himself is heaven. We are assured of success as we pursue the perfection of the acceptance of God's love, despite all the efforts of the enemies and the obstacles on the way. At the moment of our greatest desolation, we say with the Lord: "Father, into your hands I commit my spirit!"(Lk. 23:46). Then we can breathe our last on this earth in total peace.

We know that in everything God works for good with those who love him, who are called according to his purpose...What then shall we say to this? If God is for us, who is against us? He who did not spare his own Son but gave him up for us all, will he not also give us all things with him? (Rom. 8:28).

CHAPTER 8

Practicing Integration

Christian tradition tells us that to achieve a better prayer life and spiritual experience we must dispose ourselves and deliberately cultivate our interior life. St. Ignatius of Loyola speaks of spiritual exercises comparing them to physical activities.

> *"...by this name of Spiritual Exercises is meant every way of examining one's conscience, of meditating, of contemplating, of praying vocally and mentally, and of performing other spiritual actions, as will be said later. For as strolling, walking and running are bodily exercises, so every way of preparing and disposing the soul to rid itself of all the disordered tendencies, and, after it is rid, to seek and find the Divine Will as to the management of one's life for the salvation of the soul, is called a Spiritual Exercise." (Spir. Ex. #1)*

One of the most critical tasks in preparing ourselves to pray better is to quieten our mind and relax our body. Scientific psychology and Neurosciences have provided better insights into the working of our minds in the context of our brain physiology. It is not a secret that when we are physically relaxed and refreshed, our thoughts also work better. In a relaxed state of mind, we can be mindful, improve our ability to introspect and self-examine, and become more open to constructive change. In such a state of relaxation, we strengthen our intimacy and level of communication, and most importantly, we have a better chance of being entirely transparent to God in prayer. They are a scientifically informed way of achieving relaxation, a quieter mind, and body.

Training our brain:

The brain, consisting of intricate and interlocking connections of over ten billion neurons, is the physiological substratum for our perceptions, cognition, emotional functioning, learning, decision-making, etc. The brain is known to produce electromagnetic waves emanating from the myriad tiny electrical impulses that pass through the neurons. These waves are measurable through Electro-Encephalogram (EEG). The brain produces waves in different frequencies and intensities. Four types of brain-waves are of particular significance for our purposes: the Delta, Theta, Beta, and Gamma. One specific type of wave may dominate depending on the mental activity. For example in deep, dreamless, sleep the Delta is prominent. In dreamy and early waking states the Theta is dominant. As our brain is "idling" or relaxed, but awake, we produce Alpha waves. When we are actively engaging our attention to tasks, such as reading, thinking, or problem-solving, Beta is more present. In high alert situations, Gamma may be observed. An imbalance or relative absence of certain brain waves is associated with several mental conditions, such as epilepsy, attention-deficit, hyperactivity, fatigue, depression, and anxiety. When we are deeply relaxed and produce more Alpha and Theta (Alpha-Theta state) waves, we are more susceptible to change our attitudes, access and heal our memories, develop insights, etc. Recent findings suggest that lower levels of Beta (12 to 15 Hertz), known as Sensory-Motor Rhythm, are significant in improving our readiness to learn and to pay attention.

Modern Neuroscience informs us that human brain is much more changeable than was once believed. The discovery of "neuroplasticity" of the brain has inspired new experimentations in altering not only the functioning of the brain but also in seeing whether the neuronal connections themselves can be restructured. We now have convincing scientific evidence that we can deliberately train our brain to relax and to produce corresponding brain waves. For example, neurofeedback, a technique to make the brain produce more desirable brain-waves, has been found to be effective in treating specific forms of medication-resistant epilepsy. Neurofeedback also has been found to be effective in treating other brain disorders such as Attention Deficit Disorder or Hyperactivity. We can also train our brain to produce the state of relaxation that is more conducive to prayer, contemplation, and meditation. Recent research has increasingly demonstrated that mindfulness meditations effect neuro-physiological changes and prevent relapse of depression. There is now compelling scientific evidence that specific forms of prayer may significantly influence our brain-physiology as well as functioning. The question then, is: can we train the brain to help us to pray better?

History demonstrates that we instinctively feel the need to create a unique physical and psychological atmosphere for worship. We build temples, churches, mosques, and other places of worship, and elaborately design them to create an atmosphere conducive to prayer. Ritualistic cleansing of the body, fasting, abstinence, and practice of physical and mental austerity are often prescribed pre-requisites for worship; these create an internal atmosphere suitable to enter into prayer. Jesus went into the desert to fast and pray before his public ministry. Early desert-fathers, monastic traditions, and numerous lives of saints attest to the fact that the body and mind need to be brought into discipline so that the spirit can commune better with God. They were not just a practice of self-denial and personal sacrifice, but also a purification as well as physiological preparation. Many rituals of worship, such as the use of incense, chanting, symbolic expressions, vestments, candles, icons, flowers, etc. do create an enchanting atmosphere and enhance the experience of worship, albeit the fact that these were not instituted solely to create a "mood" of prayer and have other symbolic significance. We now know that these rituals and practices directly affect the functioning of the brain. Indeed, no serious objections are raised against these practices solely based on their influence on human psychology.

Spiritual Exercises and hypnotic phenomenon:

Religious trances, ritualistic worship, mystical and certain healing experiences, etc. are often associated with deep relaxation of body and mind which, in turn, is very similar to the hypnotic state. Many religious adherents object to hypnosis being associated with worship or prayer;

certainly using hypnosis as an aid to prayer. Historically, there has been some controversy regarding the nature and dynamics of hypnosis. An elaboration of these controversies is not possible in our context. The basic controversy is centered on the question whether hypnotic state is an altered state of consciousness. However, there is no disagreement in recognizing the hypnotic state as a highly focused awareness in a relaxed state of mind. It is a highly suggestible state of mind; however, there is no evidence that one can be forced to do anything against one's will while in a hypnotic state. There are considerable misconceptions of the hypnotic phenomenon among the general public, probably based on exposure to "stage hypnosis", much of which may be stage-acting for the sake of entertainment. Probably, the most prevalent and erroneous view is that hypnotic state is "unnatural" and takes away the freedom of the individual to the point of moral surrender. Hypnotic state is none other than a highly relaxed state of mind with a heightened and focused concentration. The difference between a "hypnotic state" of mind and a relaxed state of mind such as "Alpha-theta state" is not necessarily one of neurology, but of the mental disposition. In other-induced hypnosis, one is relaxing one's body and mind with a willingness to be deliberately suggestible to the hypnotist. On the contrary, in a relaxed state per se, such suggestibility is neither contracted nor willed by the subject. The deeply relaxed state of mind is open to experience without the interference of a censuring consciousness, except in situations of moral determination or threat to one's personal safety. There is no compelling scientific evidence, anecdotal narrations apart, that people can be hypnotized to do anything against their moral determinations; in fact the evidence is to the contrary. It is known that whatever the conscious mind does not object could be accepted by the subconscious as true. Children are classical examples; when a child is told that Santa Claus is coming at midnight, they accept it as true on adult-authority, because their conscious mind is not objecting to the statement. However, the moment they question it at a more mature state of mind, the veracity of the adult statement is undermined. A hypnotic state is none other than a state of mind when the critical part of the mind is set aside deliberately through deep relaxation. However, it is true that the conscious-critical mind can and will return with alacrity and reassert itself when needed, such as when a suggestion contradicting the moral position or basic security of the hypnotic subject is made. If one does not want to rob the bank, one cannot be hypnotized to rob the bank! Broadly speaking, a vast variety of human behavior on a daily basis is done under the hypnotic state, i.e. without the critical interference or questioning of the conscious mind. When we do something on "faith", such as buying milk from the grocer or allowing the barber to dress our hair or shave us, we could be considered under an uncritical state of mind, or hypnosis! We set aside unconsciously the potential that the milk could be poisoned or the barber might be a mad killer. Hypnotic state is, in this sense, one of the most commonly occurring phenomena.

Several forms of prayer, especially contemplative prayer, colloquial prayer, chanting, worshipping prayer, etc. may be in natural hypnotic, or trance-state, and rightfully so. Intimacy, especially when such is spontaneous, is often hypnotic. Hence the wise saying: "He who is aware that he is praying is not praying"! Mystical literature tells us that in "natural contemplation," at its highest manifestation, the subject cannot voluntarily end the experience of total absorption, as attested by great mystics like St. Theresa of Avila. The mystical union is pure awareness without the critical awareness interfering with it or spoiling the experience. Spiritual directors routinely advise that one should reflect on the experience of prayer after the prayer, not during! In short, many highly valued methods of prayer create a non-critical, hypnotic, state of mind, a "child-like" approach to God, fully conscious, but simple and trusting. In most ritual forms of worship, such as the liturgy of Holy Mass, certain forms of public adoration of the Eucharist, the music, the chanting, the incense, the rituals, the bells, etc. help to create a non-critical, mystical, hypnotic, alpha-theta, state of mind. With the obvious exception of discursive meditation, most meditative techniques indirectly train the subject to produce hypnotic, alpha-theta, state of mind. An example is the Taize Prayer in which short chants, repetitively sung, produces a penetrating experience of the truth that is pithily expressed in the short musical statement. The ancient saying: "He who sings prays twice" is aptly put. Some who do not understand scientific hypnosis and not realize how common-place hypnotic state of mind is, are likely to be wary or even critical of associating hypnotic state with prayer or spirituality. However, a scientific understanding of the hypnotic state of mind helps us to approach it not only with equanimity but also with the comfort of knowing that it can be used consciously to improve our prayer life and spiritual experiences. The recommendation is, therefore, obvious: do not preoccupy yourself worrying about hypnosis. You are relaxing and disposing your mind and body to be more receptive, simple, child-like, and faith-filled. You are opening your psyche to God, not going into a weird or unnatural state of mind. Your critical faculties always will be available to you when you want and need them! Do not be afraid to relax deeply at prayer for fear that you might go into hypnosis! We should review all our prayer-experiences with care; we should discern the spiritual movements and be not naïve. As was mentioned earlier (see the chapter on spiritual discernment), the fruits of our spiritual exercises require to be examined based on solid understanding of the Scripture as well as the teaching of saints and the Church. St. Ignatius of Loyola, for example, had several false visions, which he discerned as not coming from God. In hindsight, we may speculate them to have been visual hallucinations produced by psycho-physiological mechanisms, caused by extreme austerity and privations. However, as we know, he did have grand visions that were from God that changed his life and the history of the Church.

Another misunderstanding of certain forms of prayer is based on an obviously mistaken theological reasoning. Objections have been raised against certain forms of prayer, especially practiced in the Eastern cultures, stating that such are "self-centered" and "inward-looking", instead of "other-centered" and "God-centered". They argue that God is the "totally other" and should not be confused with encountering the "inner self". They insist that in prayer our goal is to experience the transcendence, "total otherness" of God and this is achieved by "looking outward". Such criticism is brought particularly against Centering Prayer and the like. Independent of justifying the method in Centering Prayer, the theological argument against it is most likely without merit. Christian prayer is an interpersonal phenomenon in faith, hope, and love. Whether one prays in consort with the community or in the privacy of one's abode, all prayer is within the psyche of the praying person. The encounter with God is *experienced* in the human subjectivity. There is no such thing as an *experience* without the subject. Prayer is, by definition, an interior affair. It is an *I-Thou* phenomenon, a dialogical stance, between the human person and God. God speaks to us in prayer, using our psyche, our awareness. Disposing our psyche to become aware of the ever-present promptings of the Spirit is the most important task of prayer. Silencing our inner chatter, and grinding the wheels of our mind to a halt, is essential. This is the experience of saints, mystics, and spiritual masters. While we look within ourselves to remove the debris, the chatter, the preoccupations, we are hoping to encounter the Lord within ourselves, in others, and indeed, in the entire creation of God. Looking deep into ourselves, to find the absence as well as the presence of God, is not self-centered!

> *Abide in me, and I in you...I am the vine; you are the branches.*
> *Whoever abides in me and I in him, he it is that bears much fruit,*
> *for apart from me you can do nothing (Jn 15:4, 5).*

The Lord abides, lives, "in you" as well as in "our midst"; look for Him first deep within yourself, by silencing your mind!

Alpha-Theta Self Training

It has been experimentally demonstrated that we can train our brain to produce Alpha-Theta waves. Such training is now available through Neuro-feedback which mostly utilizes computers and specialized machines that are designed to measure the waves and give us immediate feedback. However, it also has been demonstrated that one can train the brain without the aid of machines, albeit less efficiently. We are proposing exercises in this book without the assistance of computers. We utilize progressive relaxation through mental imagery and muscle relaxation.

Fix a time and place beforehand to do the exercise. Never do the exercise while you are driving, or operating any hazardous machinery. Find a comfortable, relaxing place to sit down, lounge, or lie down. Take the most relaxing position you prefer. Some people find it better to close their eyes to avoid visual distractions.

Step 1. Progressive muscle relaxation.

Remember relaxation is a natural response and it should happen to you if you let yourself. Relaxation occurs naturally when you deliberately remove tensions in the body. Very often we are not aware how tense we are. Muscles tense because it is ready for some sort of action or because the mind is preparing the body for work. Therefore, the first thing to do is to set aside all preoccupations and worries deliberately. At least postpone those until the exercise is done! You are about to do "nothing"! Empty your mind. Let the thoughts and feelings come and go like the waves come and go on the ocean at the whim of the wind.

Start deliberately feeling your scalp. Relax the scalp. When you try to do that, you notice that your forehead begins to relax; so do the muscles around your eyes as well as the eyelids. At this point, you can feel your eyelids wanting to close. Let them. Relax your facial muscles; let them hang, so to say. You may find that your lips are no more tightly shut. They are relaxed. You may bring on a gentle inner smile which is a relaxing posture. Now relax your neck, you may want to rest your head against a cushion on a chair or bed. Let the relaxation soon spread to your shoulders, arms, hands, and fingers. Let the arm take the most comfortable position either on your lap or your side or the armrests of a chair. Feel that they are becoming heavy and that you have no desire to move them at all. They lay there like a ton of lead. Relax your chest and all the surrounding areas. Do the same with your hip, loin area, feeling the relaxation going down to your thighs, knees, calves. Relax your feet, especially the toes. Wiggle the toes a little bit until they relax and rest naturally. Now that you feel completely relaxed, you feel very comfortable and lazy. You want to do nothing except to enjoy the peaceful state of the body. The more you relax, the more profound your relaxation!

Step 2.

Now that the body is naturally relaxing, you can pay attention to your mind. Imagine that you open the windows of your mind letting the refreshing and gentle breeze blowing away all worries and preoccupations. You allow your thoughts and feelings, no matter what they are, pass through like traffic of the mind. You have no desire to stop or examine them. You have no use judging them regarding their value or worthiness. Any thought or feeling can pass through; you could care less. Mentally you are now in a "non-active" state; allowing the mind to indulge in peace. As your physical and mental relaxation deepens, your brain is producing Alpha-theta waves. You are in the twilight zone of your awareness, neither asleep nor fully awake. The body is at rest, so is the mind. You are non-defensive and open-minded.

Step 3.

Now you are in a position to use your favorite imagery. You are in charge of your visualization as well as imagination. For example, you might visualize yourself sitting in a beautiful garden. You are carefree and can enjoy the scenery you created in your mind. See your favorite flowers in full bloom; smell the fragrance in the air. You may be sitting there in the morning, afternoon, or evening. Watch the deep blue skies, with a few white, fluffy clouds floating freely in the gentle breeze. Feel the warmth of the gentle sun on your scalp, face, and the exposed skin. Breathe in the fresh air; feel refreshed and relaxed.

If you like, you can make this into an imaginary encounter with the Lord. Imagine Him walking towards you with a smile. He comes down and sits next to you. He gives you a hug and kiss on your cheeks. You may initially want to focus on his feet. He is wearing soft leather slippers. You can see the scars of the nail-wounds on His feet. Why don't you bend down and kiss His sacred feet? See Him picking you up and seating you beside Him. You thank Him for visiting with you. You tell Him how much you want to know Him, love Him and follow Him. Stay still now and enjoy His presence.

End the exercise thanking the Lord, feeling profoundly relaxed and wholesome.

Aids to contemplative prayer:

Imaginative prayer can be very productive. St. Ignatius of Loyola has given us detailed instruction to imaginative prayer in his Spiritual Exercises. He invites us to use a scriptural event or imagined event (e.g., imagine the Lord, appearing to Blessed Mother after the resurrection and talking to her). He recommends that we might imagine being an observer or be one of the characters of the incident. Such imagination can aid us to deepen our experience of the scriptural event, assisting us to "feel and taste" (*sentire et gustare*) the experience.

In the light of clinical experience, several suggestions to improve such imaginative "contemplation" are given below. As a mnemonic aid, we shall describe them under the acronym S.M.I.L.E.

S. Use your **senses**, especially your dominant sense. See, hear, touch, smell, and taste. For example, in imagining the Wedding at Cana, you can see the dress of the Blessed Mother, the bridegroom, and the bride; hear the commotion created by the guests; listen to the chief host, loudly worrying about the situation with the wine; observe the demeanor and listen to the tone of Jesus as He is told that they have run out of wine; taste the water before it is turned into wine; taste the newly made wine; etc. The more senses we employ, the richer the experience.

M. Get into the **mood** of the narration. In the example above of the Wedding at Cana, the spirit is one of celebration. It is also an atmosphere of anxiety for the host who wants to make sure that everything goes right. Identifying with the attitude of the characters and the general atmosphere helps us to be there in spirit!

I. **Identify** with the characters of the story. Using one's imagination, one can take the role of one of the characters of the incident. For example, one can imagine being a servant, cleaning the jars and pouring water into the jars. Experience the utter surprise when the water turns into excellent wine! Or one can imagine being the water itself, being turned into wine. Experience the transformation effected by the Lord!

L. Look and visualize the more accessible aspects of the scene. For example, if you wish to imagine Jesus, focus more on his clothes, his feet or hands; not on his facial features. The face is harder to visualize than the other details of the person who you have not met before.

E. Enquire. Ask questions, both to the characters of the story as well as yourself. Interact with them. You may, for example, ask Jesus, how he felt persuaded by Mary to perform the miracle. You may talk with the Blessed Mother. You may ask the servants or the host what they were feeling and thinking of the miraculous event; nor did they even realize that it was a miracle?

CHAPTER 9

Exercises

Integrated life on a daily basis: some practical steps.

One of the most influential Doctors of the Church in modern times is St. Therese of Lisieux, popularly known as the Little Flower. Her spiritual genius demonstrated a very practical way of integrating life and attaining a deep intimacy with God and love for others. In great simplicity and honesty, Therese tackles profound and practical issues of life such as suffering, loss, and death. Above all, she teaches us how to love, serve, and remain joyful in this valley of tears. Her instructions profoundly influence many of the practical suggestions described below.

1. Total abandonment of self to God.

Trust completely in God and His love for us even as our limited intellect and warped emotions tend to tempt us to the contrary. Hold on to God as a child holds on to a father or mother in times of terror, with the certainty that unlike an earthly parent, God is capable of seeing us through any evil we might encounter. "Father, into thy hands I commit my spirit!" (Lk. 23: 46) Notice the last words of Jesus at the darkest hour of his earthly life.

"Therefore God has highly exalted him and bestowed on him the name which is above every name, that at the name of Jesus every knee should bow, in heaven and on earth and under the earth..." (Phil.2: 9-10)

Victory and salvation belong to anyone who surrenders to God's love! "What then shall we say to this? If God is for us, who is against us?" (Rom. 8:31-37)

Practice: In the morning as we wake up: "My God and my Lord, I surrender myself to you and consecrate this day to you. Sanctify this day of my life filling it with the holy presence of your Spirit of Love. I place all my trust in you my God; all my hope is in your mercy." Repeat this as often as we please during the day. End the day with a prayer similar to this: "I thank you Lord for filling this day with your loving presence, even though I may not have always been aware of your love. I place all my failures as well as victories at the foot of your cross. I rest my body and spirit in your loving bosom, knowing that you are with me always whether I am asleep or awake."

2. Experiencing God in all things and experiencing everything in God.

The *Spiritual Exercises* of St. Ignatius of Loyola culminates in a marvelous contemplation which he terms as "the contemplation to obtain love." In this exercise, Saint Ignatius invites us to experience God's presence and unfathomable love in all the creation, in all that we experience within and around us. However, this practice is not as easy as it may sound. It is not enough to know that God holds everything in being, we want to experience it! "Consider the lilies of the field, how they grow; they neither toil nor spin; yet I tell you, even Solomon in all his glory was not arrayed like one of these." (Mt. 6:28-29). Saint Francis of Assisi is the great mystic of nature where he directly experienced the glory and love of God in all his fellow creatures ("Canticle of Creation"). His spirit soared to great mystical depths as he praised and thanked the Lord for the sun, moon, stars, fellow human beings, their births, and deaths!

O Most High, all-powerful, good Lord God, to you belong praise, glory, honor, and all blessing. Be praised, my Lord, for all creation.

What we experience in our daily lives, no matter how commonplace or trivial they may appear to our tired minds, are true marvels and extraordinary in every sense. Everything we do is precious in the sight of God; our perfection is not in doing extraordinary things, but in doing ordinary things with hearts filled with love and gratitude which is the mighty "little way" of Saint Therese of Lisieux.

We naturally tend to question the presence and compassionate love of God when we encounter suffering, especially the pain of the innocent, children, the just, and the poor. We wonder how the Heavenly Father could be present in those events. Why would He permit such events? The Scripture gives several answers to this perennial question. First of all, Scripture tells us that we humans introduced suffering and death into our lives because of sin. Jesus took upon himself the consequences of all our sins by suffering and dying on the cross on our behalf. Suffering is also seen as a way of purification and testing, as gold is purified and tested in the furnace. More importantly, suffering embraced for the sake of love deepens and proves our love as the Blessed Lord, Blessed Mother, and all the saints have demonstrated. Ultimately, the mystery of suffering will remain asymptotically understood with one certainty: we live in the "valley of tears," and suffering is our constant companion on this earth. The choice is ours to use pain as an excellent source of spiritual nourishment, uniting our suffering with those of the Lord and those of the Blessed Mother. We pray continually as Saint Ignatius of Loyola prayed:

The passion of Christ, strengthen me; within Thy wounds hide me!

And again, we derive solace from the Word of God:

I consider that the sufferings of this present time are not worth comparing with the glory that is to be revealed to us...in all these things we are more than conquerors through him who loved us. (Rom 8: 18-39)

3. Forgiving ourselves as we forgive others

The pre-condition to our reaching out to God's mercy and compassion is genuine self-compassion. A lot of misunderstanding surrounds the concept of self-denial and sacrifice. Self-denial, as prescribed in the Scriptures, is consistent with self-compassion and self-care. The "denials" and abnegations are related to all those that stand in the way of our real growth and development. We indeed are not asked to be antagonistic to ourselves! We are asked to approach ourselves with the same compassion and love with which the Lord embraces us. He is delighted in our beings. We must be joyously thankful to God for giving us life and holding us in being.

All human beings, except the Blessed Mother, have fallen short of God's glory. We are all broken in one way or other. A humble recognition of this is spiritual poverty. "Blessed are the poor in spirit, for theirs is the kingdom of heaven." (Mt. 5:3) To inherit the Kingdom, we approach the Lord with our poverty and brokenness. This is the foundation of all healing. The awareness of our spiritual poverty is a deepening and life-long process. It is not our failures that determine our intimacy with God and others; it depends on how we approach God's mercy with our failures. While the evil spirit and our pride drive us to despair, the Lord invites us to the bosom of his boundless love and mercy. As we humbly kneel before the Cross and ask for forgiveness for our sins, we ask for the grace to forgive ourselves. An immediate consequence of accepting God's forgiveness and self-forgiveness is merciful forgiveness of others; in turn, the more we forgive others, the greater also our self-compassion. This goes hand in hand: "Forgive our trespasses as we forgive those who trespass against us."

4. Above all love!

Beloved, let us love one another; for love is of God, and he who loves is born of God and knows God. He who does not love does not know God; for God is love. ...if we love one another, God abides in us, and his love is perfected in us...If anyone says, "I love God," and hates his brother, he is a liar; for he who does not love his brother whom he has seen, cannot love God whom he has not seen. (1Jn. 4: 7-21)

Fill our heart and mind with love and compassion upon getting up every morning. God then lives in us truly, and He will perfect this love in us. Before we deliberate to do anything, ask ourselves: "Is this decision/action born out of genuine love?" If the answer is in the positive, then we are truly free to act! "Love and you are free to act!" this is Saint Augustine's famous dictum. The great 16th-century saint, Philip Neri, had only one rule for his followers: follow the path of love! This is the secret of all saints and the "little way" of the Little Flower. When we fill our hearts with love, an inner smile and light permeate our beings. God shines through every soul that fills itself with genuine love!

EXERCISES

Exercise 1
Keeping the House Clean

Step 1.
Deep relaxation

Step 2.
Pray to the Holy Spirit asking to purify and cleanse every aspect of my being.

Step 3.
Let the windows of my mind be open. Let the gentle breeze of the Spirit blow and cleanse my spirit and body. Let me feel His cleansing presence. Come, Lord, Holy Spirit, renew my being; conform it to the design of the Father so that in Jesus, let me become the new creation. It is no longer I who live, but Christ lives in me!

Let all anger, bitterness, lack of forgiveness, judgment, and prejudice flow out of me. Jesus, forgive me as I completely forgive those who have offended me knowingly or unknowingly. Let me love everyone as you love. Let me become your instrument of forgiveness, compassion, and love. Above all, teach me to love as Jesus loved us; this is His New Commandment: "Love one another as I have loved you."

Jesus, forgive me all my sins; blot them out as I kneel at the foot of your Cross; let me become as white as snow. Wash me clean with your precious blood; make me be born again as I bathe in the blood and water flowing from your side. Help me to receive the grace of seeing the enormity of my offenses, as even what I consider small is infinitely offensive to you. I thank you, Lord, for loving me even as I betray you; for nourishing me with your precious body and blood in the Eucharist. Let me experience the infinite depth of your love for me.

Jesus, forgive all your children. Bring your light into the darkness of those who refuse to acknowledge you, deliberately offend you, and go against you.

Step 4.

Stay still desiring to experience the cleansing by the Spirit of God. Experience the loving embrace of the Lord; experience His joy in finding the lost sheep.

Step 5.

Receive the sacrament of reconciliation, as soon as available.

Exercise 2
Daily Self Examination

Fix a place and time of the day, preferably before you go to bed. Decide how much time you will devote to the exercise, for example, ten minutes. Stick to the time allotted; do not decrease the time just because the activity does not seem to go well; do not increase the time because it is stimulating or comforting. Be faithful to your appointment.

The place and time you choose need to be adequately quiet and free from external distractions. Adopt a comfortable posture. Deeply relax your body, your mind, and your soul. Relax your body by deliberately relaxing your muscles as was taught in the "brain-training" sessions. Relax your mind by letting the thoughts and feelings come and go as the waves come and go on the ocean at the whim of the wind; do not attempt to control them or stop them; let them be; passively observe them. Set aside any preoccupations, saying to yourself that you would attend to them after the exercise. Relax your soul by surrendering all your failures and sins at the foot of the cross. Place your entire body and soul at the disposal of the Holy Spirit. Take several deep breaths and exhale slowly. Breath normally afterward.

If it helps, close your eyes.

Stay still relaxed. Pray to the Holy Spirit to enlighten you, to envelop you, to move deep within you. Imagine the Holy Spirit moving through your body, cell by cell, cleansing you, repairing and healing. Your body is His temple, His dwelling place; He keeps you breathing; in every breath you take He is present as the "Ruah," the breath of life. Imagine Him moving through your mind, driving out all evil thoughts, filling it with His seven-fold gifts. Experience His incredible love for you; how He moves you to love the Lord, to know Him more deeply and giving you the courage to follow Him more closely. Stay and enjoy the Spirit. Relax and abandon yourself to His care.

Now, gently ask Him: "Lord, help me to know myself truly, in the light of your truth, in the way you see me." Stay still! Do not answer for Him.

He will let you become aware of His holy silence which speaks louder than any words. His ways are not your ways; His way of making you know is not how you imagine it. Let Him do it in His way. He will let you become aware of the obstacles that stand in His way into you. He loves you; do not be anxious!

You may choose to go through each activity of the day hour by hour or event by event as if you are watching a video of yourself. Become mindful how God was present. Focus more on the feeling how much God loved you throughout the day; how your guardian angel protected you. Ask forgiveness, if you were not following His will, if you neglected the promptings of the Holy Spirit.

End the exercise by thanking and praising the Lord.

Exercise 3
Establishing a place of consultation

Everyone needs to consult, to seek advice, and above all to pray to God for the gift of discernment and guidance. It may be good practice to establish a protocol, especially for the latter. There are times you may want to pray to the Holy Spirit; at other times you may desire to be with the Blessed Mother; many people have conversations with their guardian angels as consultants. In this exercise, one establishes a pre-determined atmosphere for this prayer of "consultancy." The actual physical location of the prayer of "consultancy" may be one's room, a chapel, or even under a favorite tree in the garden. However, in this exercise, one is establishing a "place" or atmosphere of one's creation by imagination. Once established, one returns to this "place" whenever there is need to consult or discern.

Step 1.
Deeply relax and pray to the Holy Spirit to guide you through this exercise. "Lord, help me to establish in my mind, through my creative imagination, a place where I can meet with you in prayer to consult with you when I need special guidance..."

Step 2.
Creatively imagine a place or atmosphere that you feel comfortable to be with the Lord. Some have decided to find a "consulting room" in heaven, an elegantly decorated room with a comfortable sofa, heavenly, soft, background music, etc.; others may choose a corner of an elegant Cathedral where it is quiet and spiritual, yet others might prefer a garden or a beach, etc.

Step 3.
Having decided on a "location," you construct the details of the atmosphere. No rules of construction here! However, it must be conducive to private consultation and worthy of the presence of God or His saints.

Step 4.

Having constructed the atmosphere, familiarize yourself thoroughly with it, taking your time to sit there alone. You might pray to the Holy Spirit to bless the atmosphere.

Step 5.

Establish a "key" to the place in your mind. The "key" could be a short prayer, such as "I need to consult in prayer." "Veni Sancte Spiritu," "Jesus I need to check with you"... When you say this with the desire to consult in prayer, you will be, in your imagination, "transported" instantly to the "place." You will not have to go through examining or elaborating the details of the room again. You will be relaxed, hopeful, and filled with the joy of consulting with the Lord.

Step 6.

When you have an actual need to discern something significant before the Lord, make an appointment with the Lord, or the saint or angel you want to consult with for a specific time of the day. Go to the chapel or your room or any other comfortable, distraction-free place and use the "key" to transport yourself to the "consultancy place." Your guest will already be there!

Exercise 4

Discernment before making decision

St. Ignatius of Loyola, the master of spiritual discernment, provides several methods of discernment before making a serious decision. In the most commonly practiced procedure, we are asked to carefully consider the pros and cons of a potential resolution and weigh them and discern their merits in prayer to arrive at a decision. This process might appear to be deceptively simple; experience tells us otherwise. It is doubly difficult when we are forced to choose between two non-desirable outcomes or between two good choices. Sometimes it is easier to follow God's will than to know what it is! In this exercise, we prepare ourselves so that we are helped to discern God's will in difficult-to-know situations.

Deeply relax.

Following St. Ignatius's guidance, imagine yourself prostrate before the most holy Trinity. Imagine the glorious presence of the Blessed Mother, the angelic court, and the saints. Before this most august assembly, you kneel and prostrate in great reverence and humility.

Offer a prayer of petition somewhat similar to this:

"Father, Son and Holy Spirit, I prostrate before you, your humble creature, totally in need of your loving assistance. I acknowledge my total dependence on you. I come to you transparent, poor in heart, trusting in your love, mercy, and goodness. Do not consider my unworthiness, but consider the faith and great fidelity of our heavenly Mother, the most Blessed Virgin. Consider the faith of all your saints and your Church. Be pleased with the presence of all the holy angels who you assigned as our guardians and protectors throughout our lives. I come to you to grant me the wisdom and gift of discernment. Help me so that I can know your will. Give me the courage to follow your will; because I know your will is the best for me. Let my decision be for your greater glory, for the good of all, and for my salvation and sanctification. I know whatever I ask in the name of the Lord will be granted me according to your holy

will. In all humility and trust, I ask this favor in the name of the Lord Jesus Christ. Lord, be merciful and kind to me!"

Stay quiet after the prayer as long as you please.

Clarify in your mind regarding your choices. Make it as specific as you can. What are the possible decisions you are facing? Eliminate forthwith from your mind any alternative that is apparently wrong or morally reprehensible; they are not worthy of consideration!

Gently bring to your awareness your natural predisposition to choose one over the other. Become aware of your personal bias without self-recrimination or criticism. Your preference is your bias. Acknowledge and accept it as such. Once you are aware of this, say: "Lord, you know this is my bias, my inclination. Thank you for letting me become aware of it. But not my will, but yours will be done."

Bring to your mind the cons for the choices you prefer or if you have no preference, consider the arguments for one of the options.

Now consider the arguments against that possible decision.

Consider all the choices before you in this manner.

Consider the choice you are likely to make and examine it more closely. Does that increase your faith, hope, and love? If you made this choice, can you see yourself happy with the Lord, yourself and others?

Present the choice that you have made before the Lord and pray that He blesses your choice.

If you are still not decided or happy, consult someone you consider wise and unbiased.

Exercise 5
Achieving a goal

Deeply relax!

In a relaxed state of body, mind, and soul you clarify and select one specific goal, spiritual or temporal, that you want to achieve.

Gently observe how much you desire this goal. Increase the desire until you el emotionally charged with energy towards the goal.

Clarify to yourself why you desire this goal so much. How important is this goal for you?

Ask the Holy Spirit to purify your desire for this goal. Does He want you to achieve this goal? Will this goal glorify the Lord, serve others, build the Lord's Kingdom, and fulfill you?

Having clarified the above, how much confidence you have in the Lord and yourself as His instrument, in achieving this goal? Pray for courage and self-efficacy.

Imagine the means by which you can achieve this goal. Pray to the Holy Spirit to give you discipline, courage, perseverance, and insight to adopt the methods.

Figure out what you need to do to achieve this goal.

Figure out how you will collaborate with others or elicit others' help in achieving this goal?

Imagine that you have achieved the goal. When and where? How do you feel having achieved the goal?

Decide to move forward. Ask the Lord to be with you. Pray for assistance to the Blessed Mother and your favorite saints. Ask the guardian angel to be with you.

End the exercise by thanking the Lord.

Exercise 6
Overcoming a spiritual obstacle or challenge

The beginning is the same as in Exercise 5. Go into a deeply relaxed state of body and mind.

Gently bring to mind an obstacle that you encounter more frequently than others. For example, you don't choose to find time for personal prayer; you may have a particular and persistent feeling of antipathy towards a person; you may have difficulty accepting an order from your superior; etc. Just pick one issue. It does not even have to be the most important. Let the Lord inspire you to pick one.

Having fixed your mind on one obstacle, acknowledge it in peace and make it your goal to overcome it through this exercise.

Imagine that you are sitting on a sandy shore of the Sea of Galilee. It is your imagination; you can make up the scene as it occurs in your mind. There are no rules! For example, it is towards evening, the floating patches of clouds above the deep blue sky are already picking colors from the setting sun, gold, amber, and pink. Feel the gentle evening breeze cooling you to a deeply relaxed state. Watch the waves as they come and go at the whim of the wind. Listen to the birds as they wind up the day's work. It is so peaceful and relaxing! Imagine that the Lord is sitting next to you on the clean sand. He is playing with the dry sand, scooping up the sand in His sacred hands, letting it sift through his fingers. Look at the glorious satin cloak The Lord is wearing; it reaches all the way to his feet. You can see his bare feet. Observe the nail-scars of crucifixion on them. Feel His gentle and everlasting love for you. He is asking you: "Do you love me?" You answer Him: "Lord, you know that I love you." Enjoy His silence. You then tell Him: "Lord, I have this problem, this obstacle that I encounter. It grieves me and annoys me. Please help me." Stay quiet. Know in your heart that He wants to heal you; he wants you to succeed. You thank him for wanting to help you. You tell him that you will dispose yourself, so that he can heal you.

Increase your desire in your heart to overcome the obstacle.

Figure out what you need to do to overcome the challenge. What means can you adopt? How can you dispose your mind to adopt the means? Clarify the concrete steps.

Ask the Lord to give you courage and perseverance. You tell him that you know that progress is not linear or straight up; you are aware that the road to success may be winding, though upwards. You will get up, as he did on the way to the Cross when you fall without discouragement or surrender. You also ask him, if it is his will, to cure you as fast as possible. Surrender your thoughts to him. End with a prayer of thanksgiving. "Lord, you told us that you had conquered the world; you have conquered all evil, including death. I place all my trust in you."

Exercise 7

A method of contemplating an incident in the Scripture (adapted from the Spiritual Exercises of St. Ignatius Loyola).

Step 1.
Follow the steps in the foundational exercise to relax the mind and body.

Step 2.
Pray to the Holy Spirit to assist you through the exercise

Step 3.
Pray to the Evangelist (e.g., St. John) for assistance

Step 4.
Read the passage of the Gospel attentively and slowly (e.g., Jn, 9)

Step 5.
Pick one or a group of characters in the incident (e.g., the blind man, his parents, the Pharisee, or create a character, e.g., an observer). Identify yourself with that character or group.

Step 6.
Visualize the scene. Take as much time as possible. Go into the details, such as being on a hillside; see the shrubberies; pick some wild berries and taste them; feel the warmth or heat of the sun; visualize the sky, the white or dark clouds; listen to the birds; smell the air, etc. etc.

Step 7.
Observe the characters in the story. For example, observe the blind man; see what he is wearing; see his disheveled hair, dusty feet, dirty hands, etc. Observe his parents among the crowd. Observe Jesus arriving at the scene with his disciples. Listen to the disciples asking the Lord: "Rabbi, who sinned, this man or his parents? Listen to Jesus answering them (if

necessary go back and read the sentences from the scripture. Observe what Jesus is doing to cure the man of his blindness...observe what happens next...etc. (The idea is for you to experience the entire event as though you were there. Soak in the scene visually and through all your senses)

Step 8.
Feel what you are feeling. Let the feelings come and go. Deepen the feelings.

Step 9.
Ask the Lord to touch your heart and mind. Stay still! Let Him do what He wants to do.

Step 10.
End the exercise thanking the Lord for breaking His Word for you and nourishing you.

Step 11.
After the exercise, you may want to write down your reflections on the activity.

Exercise 8

A method of discursive meditation on a scripture passage

Step 1.

Same as the foundational exercise

Step 2.

Select a passage from the scripture that you want to meditate on

Step 3.

Pray to the Holy Spirit for His grace and the human author of the scripture passage for assistance (e.g., St. Paul)

Step 4.

Read the scripture slowly and attentively

(Below I give a scripture passage as an example)

Jn. 16: 4-15

> ---*I did not say these things to you from the beginning, because I was with you. But now I am going to him who sent me; yet none of you asks me, 'where are you going?' But because I have said these things to you, sorrow has filled your hearts. Nevertheless, I tell you the truth: it is to your advantage that I go away, for if I do not go away, the Counselor will not come to you; but if I go, I will send him to you. And when he comes, he will convince the world of sin and righteousness and judgment: of sin, because they do not believe in me; of righteousness, because I go to the Father, and you will see me no more; of judgment because the ruler of this world is judged.*
>
> *I have yet many things to say to you, but you cannot bear them now. When the Spirit of truth comes, he will guide you into all the truth; for he will not speak on his authority, but whatever he hears he will speak, and he will declare to you the things that are to come. He will glorify me, for he will take what is mine and declare*

it to you. All the Father has is mine, therefore, I said that he will take what is mine and declare it to you. (Jn. 16:4-15)

Understand the context. (e.g., the passage above is part of the great discourse at the Last Supper, narrated by John.) Imagine that you are sitting in the corner of the upper room listening to what Jesus is saying.

Pick a theme of the passage that strikes you (e.g., in the above passage, you can pick the topic of the relationship between the three persons of the most Holy Trinity; or the theme of why Jesus, of necessity, has to "go away" so that the Holy Spirit can come, etc.) Pick only one idea at a time!

For example, let us stick to why Jesus says that he has to go away.

Why is it that Jesus did not stick around "physically" after the resurrection? Wouldn't it have been great fun, if he kept appearing on and off as he did for "forty days" after the resurrection? What is the point of his ascension? If he did not go away, we could call on him to consult with him when we are in trouble; we could show off Jesus physically to those who don't believe in him; we could ask his help directly during great troubles; etc. Why is it that Jesus and the Holy Spirit can't be "working together" on this post-resurrection era? Why seemingly "only" one person at a time?

Stay with the questions. Observe how you feel. How do you like God's plan? Do you find joy or sorrow or a mixture of feelings? How do you surrender to God's plan as He revealed it? If He consulted you, how would you have advised Him? Why are God's ways so different from those of ours?

Stay still. Pray to Jesus spontaneously. For example: "Lord why did you not stay physically with us? Why did you have to ascend? Why can't Holy Spirit descend on us while you were still with us physically? Help me to understand this? What does it mean for me? …"

Step 5.

End with a spontaneous prayer of surrender to God. Example: "Lord, your ways are not mine. I surrender myself to you; your wisdom, your love; because you are all knowing, wisdom itself. Have mercy on me."

Exercise 9

A meditation to increase faith:

Step 1.

Deep relaxation

Step 2.

Imagine yourself sitting on a sandy beach of the Sea of Galilee. It is your imagination! Create the scene the way you like it. Visualize the scenery: clean, dry sand, a few rocks on the side, shrubbery growing on the sides. Watch the broken sea-shells. Watch the gentle waves, glimmering in the evening sun. Watch the deep blue sky, the few fluffy white clouds freely floating in the air, picking up hues from the evening sun. Listen to the sound of the waves, the birds flying around looking for an evening meal before they retire. Feel the gentle evening breeze on your face, cooling your body comfortably. Breath in the fresh air, taste the subtle taste of salt in the air. Smell the evening air, pleasant and natural…You are seated on the shore facing the sea; you are the only one there. You know that Jesus once walked on this shore. He walked on these waters. He calmed the sea. He cooked breakfast for the disciples and fed them fire roasted fish after his resurrection. You wish with all your heart that the Risen Lord visits you there!

Step 3.

Pray. "Jesus, my Lord and my God, come and be my side. I want you to increase my faith in you. Breathe your Spirit into me. Strengthen me in my faith in you…"

Step 4.

Imagine that Jesus is sitting beside you! He is patting you on your shoulders with his sacred hands. Feel his comforting and loving touch. Watch his white tunic reaching almost to his feet. Touch it and feel its smooth texture. Observe his sacred feet. The scars of the nails are still there. Why don't you kneel down and kiss his sacred feet and the precious scars. Feel his touch on your head, blessing you with unfathomable love and willingness. Pray: "I adore you my Lord, and my God. I worship you with all my heart. Remove all hesitations and doubts from my mind; deepen my commitment to you; my faith in you! Let me never be diminished in my faith."

Step 5.

Quieten your mind and heart. Feel the infusion of faith. Slowly recite the Apostles' Creed. Stay with any phrase or article that strikes you. For example, you may stay and deepen your understanding of the mystery of the incarnation. The Lord is indeed God the Son, the Word of God, who gives meaning and existence to everything that is. He indeed became a man, met us in flesh and blood; became part of our history. He is the God-initiated answer to all human longing for God. I do not need to look anywhere else. He is indeed the meaning of my life; he is the answer to my entire quest.

Step 6.

"Jesus you call me by my name. You know me more than I know myself. I am utterly transparent before you; I cannot hide from you. Come, Lord, abide in me; be the Self of my self; the heart of my heart. You are my life, my hope forever. You love me more than I can imagine. I want to believe in you; love you, and follow you ever more closely…"

Step 7.

Thank the Lord for visiting you. End the exercise, knowing that Jesus truly visited you in the activity, even though you started it as your imagination, a wish. Jesus indeed is present to you all the time! That is the real truth of faith. He is truly there when you sincerely call upon him.

Exercise 10

A meditation to increase Hope in times of trial:

Step 1.

Deep relaxation

Step 2.

In your imagination transport yourself to the garden of Gethsemane. Imagine the time of day or night. Use your senses in your imagination to experience the garden. Remind yourself that the Lord went through His agony in this very place.

Step 3.

Pray to the Lord to bless your exercise and send His Holy Spirit. "Lord, I come to you at the very place where you went through the agony before your "descent into hell." I am in a trial; I know my trial is small compared to what you went through. But I know you care for me deeply; you care what happens to me, no matter how small. You are present in the tiniest blade of grass, as you are present in the large galaxies. In your eyes, there is nothing small or big! They all fit in the palm of your hands. Hold me in the palm of your hands. Look at me struggling. Give me hope and courage. Talk to me and say again: Do not be afraid!"

Stay still.

Step 4.

Converse with Jesus; describe to him the details of your strife and conflict. Tell him how you feel. Stay quiet after you are done. Feel his compassion and willingness to help you. If it helps, place your head at his feet as Mary Magdalene did at the house of Simon.

Step 5.

Transport yourself in your imagination to the entrance of the Empty Tomb. Use your senses to be there! The Lord has risen; the tomb is empty! Pray: "Lord, you appeared to Mary Magdalene and called her by her name. I come to you filled with hope that you will also call me by my name. Help me to feel your presence; fill me with the hope that this trial of mine will also pass; comfort me! I know you will call me by name and fill me with your glorious joy. I place all my trust in you! Have mercy on me..."

Exercise 11

Accessing the Divine Counselor: a contemplative exercise in discernment

Holy Spirit is always with us. He is the promised Counselor, the Advocate, who guides the Church and us until the end of time. He dwells deep within, teaching us how to pray.

Step 1.
Deep relaxation

Step 2.
Pray to the Holy Spirit. You may use the chant repetitively: "Veni Sancte Spiritu" or "Come Holy Spirit!" Feel the presence of the Spirit or wish sincerely to feel His presence.

Step 3.
"Lord Holy Spirit, I adore and worship you; you are my helper, my advocate, my comforter, as promised by Jesus. I know that you are always present. I long to feel your presence. I need you now more than ever to guide and direct me. I am coming to you with a specific need; please guide me in the right direction; help me to discern your will; give me the wisdom and courage to follow your light…"

Bring to the Lord the specific issue with which you are dealing. Talk audibly, if it helps, to the Lord as openly as you can without fear, knowing that the Lord knows your innermost self and you are utterly transparent to him. After you talked, be still. You may repeatedly chant *Veni Sancte Spiritu*.

Step 4.
Consider the choice you feel the wisest. Present it to the Lord. Observe how you feel. Do you feel closer to the Lord, as you consider making that choice? Is your love for others increased? Are you at peace with the choice? Consider every fruit of the Spirit and see how your decision could be related to them, positively or negatively…Is the Lord asking you to postpone the

decision? Is He guiding you to talk to someone, your superior, spiritual director, a friend..?

Step 5.
Make a choice temporarily knowing that you can change your mind if the Lord guides you in another direction. Ask the Lord to bless and approve your decision. Thank him for helping you.

Step 6.
End the exercise with a prayer of adoration and thanksgiving.

Step 7.
If circumstances allow, carry the decision with you for a few days; repeatedly present the choice to the Lord in short periods of prayer. Observe how the Spirit moves you. Are you consoled or desolate?

Step 8.
If you feel confirmed, stick with the decision and surrender it to the Lord trusting in Him. If you do not feel confirmed, take the next best choice and repeat the process, until you feel confirmed.

Exercise 12

A lesson from the Master Himself on Christian love

Step 1.

Deep relaxation

Step 2.

Read Jn. 13:34-35

A new commandment I give to you, that you love one another: Just as I have loved you, you also are to love one another. By this, all people will know that you are my disciplesif you have love for one another.

Step 3.

Imagine that you have an appointment with Jesus; upon your request, he has agreed to give you this appointment (you can choose the place of meeting at your will; for example: on the shore of the Sea of Galilee). You imagine that you got their half an hour earlier. Visualize the scene; use all your senses to make the place as real as possible. Pray with great longing for the Lord to appear. You want him to explain the meaning and implications of the passage.

Step 4.

The Lord appears at the exact appointed time. Adore Him, fall at His side. You tell Him that you would sit at His feet as in ancient times a student lay at the feet of his master.

Step 5.

You reread the passage.

A new commandment I give to you, that you love one another:

Just as I have loved you, you also are to love one another. By this, all people will know that you are my disciples if you have love for one another.

Step 6.

Ask the Lord, these and similar questions: Why is this a *New* commandment? What is the distinguishing mark of the Christian love? How is this different from "Love thy neighbor as yourself"? Stay with the questions. The questions are the most important; the answers keep coming, it never ends!

> *"Lord, your word is unfathomable; I will never reach the full understanding of it. You continue to nourish me with it, as I need it. Let me live by your word, as it is broken to me every day of my life. Praise and thanksgiving to you, my Lord and my God!"*

Step 7.

End the meditation with personal prayer.

Exercise 13
Walk in the Spirit

> *"Likewise the Spirit helps us in our weakness; for we do not know how to pray as we ought, but the Spirit himself intercedes for us with sighs too deep for words. And he who searches the hearts of men knows what is the mind of the Spirit because the Spirit intercedes for the saints according to the will of God." (Rom. 8:26)*

Taking a walk every day is a good thing from many points of view. We can pray while we walk.

Prayer before starting:

> *"Come Holy Spirit, renew my life. Envelop my being with the warmth of your unfathomable love. Let me experience the fruits of your holy presence in my life: love joy, peace, patience, kindness, goodness, faithfulness, gentleness, self-control (Gal. 5:22) Let me walk with you! Every breath I take, every step I take, let your saving and refreshing energy quicken me. Come into me as I take every breath; purify me as I exhale. Come Holy Spirit, renew my life!"*

As you start your walk, keep repeating the prayer: "Come Holy Spirit, renew my life!"

As you focus on the chant, imagine and experience the presence of the Lord, filling your body, mind, and soul. The truth is He is enveloping you with His Grace.

As you look around, see the Spirit of God at work in everything you see and encounter.

As you end the walk, take a moment and thank the Holy Spirit. Say a prayer somewhat like this:

> *"Spirit of God, together with the Father and the Son, you are the Self of my self, the ground of my being. You build your Kingdom deep within me and in our midst. Let me love you above all; let me*

love all your creation, as you delight in it. I thank you, Lord, for always being with me."

Exercise 14
A Meditation for healing the body

Our body is made to heal itself when illness afflicts us or when we are injured. The medicines we take are to assist the body in its healing work; drugs do not cure, the body does. We believe in the Spirit of life. The Holy Spirit is the life principle that keeps us alive and well. This meditation is to deepen our awareness of the healing presence of the Spirit and to pray to the Holy Spirit for our healing.

Step 1.
Deeply relax your body and mind

Step 2.
Start with the prayer:

> *"Come, Holy Spirit, comforter of my soul, healer of my being, Life of my life! Come and renew my being. You made me in your image; come and heal me according to your holy will."*

Stay with the prayer as long as you like.

Step 3.
Focus on the area of injury, or on the sensations of the body making you feel ill. Imagine that the Holy Spirit is sending the warmth of His healing power throughout the region of your injury, or through your entire body. Try to feel the warmth of His presence, enveloping you like a warm blanket on a chilly day.

> *"Spirit of God, Life of my life, please repair my body and my soul with your anointing love. You are the source of all life; you are my renewal; you are my health and wellbeing. Without you I perish, I return to the dust from which I came. Cleanse me in my body and soul. Remove everything that stands in your way. Straighten my path; let me turn completely towards you. I unite my suffering with those of my Lord, who suffered every injury and death for my*

salvation. Let my suffering be not a waste, but be made precious in your sight, purifying me and building the Church."

Step 4.
Rest as long as you please in the presence of the Spirit moving through you, enveloping you with love.

Step 5.
End the exercise thanking the Holy Spirit for healing you. Trust in Him and entrust your entire body and soul to Him.

Exercise 15
Healing the trauma of childhood sexual abuse

Some of us have the unfortunate experience of being sexually abused in childhood. Sexual encounters with children of the same age usually have a less deleterious effect than abuse by adults. The traumatic impact will vary depending on several factors, including the manner and circumstances in which the violation occurred, the relationship of the perpetrator to the victim, the psychological status of the victim, etc. The impact of incest is usually different from the victimization by a stranger. At any rate, sexual abuse may seriously affect the psychological and spiritual life of the victim. Some may develop Post Traumatic Stress Disorder, chronic depression, anxiety-conditions, sexual conflicts, behavioral disorders, etc. Competent professional intervention may become necessary if the condition remains persistent. The following exercise is not meant to be a substitute for appropriate professional and spiritual help.

Traumatic experiences, by definition, are experiences that overwhelm the usual coping mechanisms of the person and tend to become difficult to assimilate. The treatment approaches primarily employ methods of assimilation through desensitization and restructuring of the experience, both cognitively and regarding behavioral responses, in a relaxed frame of mind and body.

Step 1.

Find a comfortable, private time and location. This exercise is best performed in one's private room. Appoint the time ahead and make sure you give enough time (at least an hour) to complete the exercise. Also make sure that you don't have anything significant to do, especially in collaboration with others, immediately after the practice.

Your body and mind should be in a relaxed and pain-free state, if possible.

Repeat the exercise a few times, until the restructuring of the traumatic experience happens.

Step 2.

Deeply relax and achieve an Alpha-Theta state of mind.

Step 3.

Pray to the Holy Spirit to assist you in this healing exercise.

> *"Come, Holy Spirit, comforter, and counselor, healer, and giver of life! You are the promised Advocate, the Paraclete. Come and renew my life; heal my body and soul..."*

Try to experience the presence of the Holy Spirit. Entrust your life to Him.

Steps 4.

Relaxedly bring to mind the sexual trauma, as if you are hearing the story from a child, the child you were at the time of the incident. Be mindful. Do not judge yourself or find fault with yourself. If you feel upset or angry at the perpetrator, let the feelings come and go.

Observe the feelings. Identify them. Relax your mind and body as you observe them.

Become aware of your age now. You are an adult (or more grown up than when you experienced the event). Say: "I am here alive and wiser. I have survived the trauma. I can get my life back if I choose to.

Go back to the scene as you are now, wiser, more mature, and better equipped to handle the situation. Tell the perpetrator:

> *"What you have done is wrong and harmful. You did not consider my welfare or future. I was a child when you did this to me. I know better now. If I knew what I know now, I wouldn't have allowed you to do this to me. I know I was confused when this happened to me. I am letting you go from my mind and heart; I will not allow you to intrude into me anymore. May God have mercy on you!"*

Now pray:

> *"Lord, I surrender this experience at the foot of your Cross. I aban-*
> *don it and refuse to hold on to it. I refuse to carry any guilt associ-*
> *ated with it. I declare myself free of this experience once and for all.*
> *God wants me to let it go. He is carrying it away for me, from me.*
> *I declare myself free, clean, and wholesome with the help of God.*
> *He has cleansed me and healed me from this horrible experience;*
> *He has freed me from its consequence. Let the experience become*
> *truly a past event; let it not have any adverse impact on my present*
> *or future life. Lord Jesus, forgive me all my sins; wash me clean of*
> *all bad experiences. Let my body and soul become truly a dwelling*
> *place for you..."*

Step 5.

Imagine yourself sitting on the grass in a lovely garden; visualize the surrounding to your liking. Employ all your senses. Feel the warmth of the
sun, the gentle breeze, smell the blooming flowers, listen to the birds sing-
ing, look at the deep blue sky with a few white, fluffy clouds floating freely,
picking up colors from the sun…Now feel the freedom the Lord has given
you; experience the healing that he has achieved in you. Feel grateful,
happy, having let go of your burden. Feel light, cleansed, filled with the joy
of the Spirit. Some find it consoling to imagine that Jesus is sitting by their
side. They imagine that the Lord is asking them to forget the past, focus on
the present and future; that He loves them more than ever.

Step 6.

Bring back the bad memory. Recognize it as such, just a memory of a bad
experience. See that it has no impact on you anymore. A memory is only
in mind. It is not anymore present. It does not have to have any effect on
your future, your choices, or enjoyment of life. You are as good as new in
the eyes of the Lord, in your eyes.

"Behold, I make everything new!" Hear the Lord's words.

Step 7.

End the exercise, with a clear resolution: whenever the memory of this event intrudes into my mind, I will automatically say: "It is past, it is gone. The Lord has healed me; I am free." And relaxedly let it go from your mind. Thank the Lord for His everlasting love for you as you end the exercise.

CHAPTER 10

Experiencing God in all things: The spirituality of the laity for the 21st century

"To be holy does not require being a bishop, a priest or a religious. We are frequently tempted to think that holiness is only for those who can withdraw from ordinary affairs to spend much time in prayer. This is not the case. We are called to be holy by living our lives with love and by bearing witness in everything we do, wherever we find ourselves..." (Pope Francis: Gaudete et exsultate: #14)

There are relatively very few lay faithful who have occupied the roster of canonized saints. This has given an implicit and false impression that heroic holiness is more difficult for those who have been called outside of the ministerial priesthood, monastic and religious life. Somehow the heroic and sacrificial life of lay people has gone without the type of acclaim and adulation that it truly deserves. The vast majority of the People of God is laity. They are called to live in this world, fully engaged with it, being the light of the world. "They are the Church" (Ref. Catechism of the Catholic Church #899). The sacrament of marriage and family life creates the fundamental unit of the Church, the "domestic church". It is the primary and foundational place of evangelization; for most of the faithful, faith is primarily transmitted and cultivated in the loving atmosphere of the family. The Christian family demonstrates analogously the movement of the Three-personal love of God. It is in Christian matrimony, the real love of Christ for the Church is sacramentally made visible. Through their baptism and confirmation, the laity are anointed and integrated into the People of God, and are made sharers in the priestly, prophetic, and kingly office of Christ (Catechism #898). The lay faithful are equal in dignity and membership in the Body of Christ, the Church. The Church reflects its holiness and struggles through the lives of the lay people. "You, therefore, must be perfect, as your heavenly Father is perfect," (Mt. 5:48; Col. 1:28) is indeed addressed to ALL who follow Christ.

> "Because of their special vocation, it belongs to the laity to seek the kingdom of God by engaging in temporal affairs and directing them according to God's will. . . . It particularly pertains to them so to illuminate and order all temporal things with which they are closely associated..." (Catechism of the Catholic Church #897)

The following proposals are practical ways of living a life of simple spirituality as lay faithful, especially those who are leading a family life.

> "May the Lord make you increase and abound in love to one another and all men, as we do to you, so that he may establish your hearts unblamable in holiness before our God and Father, at the coming of our Lord Jesus with all his saints" (Ths. 3: 12)

Holiness does not consist in doing extraordinary things, but in living "ordinary" life with faith, hope, and charity. Sanctity is God's pure gift to us, not the result of our efforts. Our efforts do not achieve perfection; it consists in how much we let ourselves be perfected in Christ, by uniting ourselves with him. The Lord declares blessed those who experience the need of God continually in their lives (the poor in spirit) and place their trust in Him. The Kingdom of God belongs to those who depend on God for their movement towards completeness (perfection) in Christ (Col.1:28).

Step 1.

Believe and recognize that I am called by God to lead a family life. God has already blessed me with all the extraordinary grace and the means that I need to conduct a heroically holy life in conformity with the Lord's will. If I cooperate, what God has started in my Baptism, He will bring to a glorious conclusion for me.

My constant prayer is "Thy will be done ON EARTH as it is in heaven." While my gaze is on my eternal life with God, my efforts are to start building the Kingdom on this EARTH. Jesus is in our midst! "Today this scripture has been fulfilled in your hearing."(Lk.4:21). Heaven and hell start here on earth!

Step 2.

When I wake up in the morning, the first thing I do is to praise and thank the Lord and ask for His grace to dedicate the day to Him and to spend the day entirely in conformity to His Spirit. I humbly implore the Lord that He sanctifies the day. I take a moment to gather myself and resolve with God's grace to be mindful in all that I choose and do today.

Step 3.

I bring to my mind every member of my household, my husband/wife, children, and others that live and work in my home; I love them in my heart and decide to pour myself out for them in loving service. Let me be attentive, kind, generous, self-less…with all the members of my family. I respect, love, and cherish my spouse, as Christ loves the Church. I shall be attentive to my children with mindfulness, often asking myself what I need to do for them.

> *"In a very special way, parents share in the office of sanctifying "by leading a conjugal life in the Christian spirit and by seeing to the Christian education of their children."(Catechism #902)*

Step 4.

I choose, as much as possible, to be mindful of God's loving presence in me, in all those whom I meet today, and in every event I encounter today. I see God in everything and everything through God. I choose a very short prayer that I shall often say today, such as: "Spirit of God, be my light!" "Jesus, I love you!" "Lord, have mercy!" "Jesus, Mary, Joseph," etc.

When conflicts arise, I try to center myself and ask the Lord for guidance in the spirit of love. "Let me love as You have loved!"

When I am tempted to do something I know to be wrong, I pray: "Lord, deliver me from all evil."

If I do go wrong, I return as soon as possible to the Lord, asking for his healing and forgiveness.

Step 5.

I refuse to harbor any malice, or wish evil upon anyone; even those who I know have hurt me with malice. While I courageously assert myself against what is not right and call evil by its name, I ask for the grace of forgiveness to those who harm me. As a parent, I dare to lovingly correct those who are in my care with patience and forbearance, knowing in my heart that at the end love will conquer all evil.

Step 6.

In the work-place, I shall put forth my best effort, producing and contributing my best. I peacefully recognize that there are many ways of accomplishing a goal. While I let my opinions be known as appropriate, I shall submit to the legitimate authority and decision-making responsibility of my superiors. I shall encourage and support my co-workers with Christian love and generosity. I shall respect and treat kindly those who work for me, always recognizing the dignity of their personhood and their work.

> "Lay believers are in the front line of Church life; for them, the Church is the animating principle of human society. Therefore, they, in particular, ought to have an ever-clearer consciousness not only of belonging to the Church but of being the Church. And so, worshipping everywhere by their holy actions, the laity consecrate the world itself to God, everywhere offering worship by the holiness of their lives." (Catechism of the Catholic Church #899)

If I am housebound as a mother or father, I shall do everything keeping love in my heart as the Blessed Mother did.

Step 7.

In the evening I shall pray together with my family.

Step 8.

At the end of the day, I shall take a few moments to gather myself in quiet to thank the Lord for all that happened during the day and asking for forgiveness for the wrongs I might have done.

Step 9.

I shall, together with my family, worship the Lord at the Eucharistic celebration at least on Sundays.

> *"Hence the laity, dedicated as they are to Christ and anointed by the Holy Spirit, are marvelously called and prepared so that even richer fruits of the Spirit maybe produced in them. For all their works, prayers, and apostolic undertakings, family and married life, daily work, relaxation of mind and body, if they are accomplished in the Spirit - indeed even the hardships of life if patiently born - all these become spiritual sacrifices acceptable to God through Jesus Christ. In the celebration of the Eucharist, these may most fittingly be offered to the Father along with the body of the Lord. And so, worshipping everywhere by their holy actions, the laity consecrate the world itself to God, everywhere offering worship by the holiness of their lives." (Catechism #901)*

Step 10.

I shall contribute my time and treasure towards the community as much as I can, always keeping in mind that it is my Christian duty to assist especially the poor and the underprivileged (Mt. 25: 35-40).

These practices may appear to be deceptively simple as we read them; however, the actual implementation will be possible only with God's assistance which fortunately is guaranteed to us as long as we are willing to receive and cooperate with it.

> *"Not that I have already obtained this or am already perfect; but I press on to make it my own because Christ Jesus has made me his …press on toward the goal for the prize of the upward call of God in Christ Jesus." (Phil. 3:12-14)*

A.M.D.G.